Al-Wala' wa'l-Bara'

According to the 'Aqeedah of the Salaf

Muhammad Saeed al-Qahtani

PART 3

The Meaning of Wala' and Bara'

Al-Firdous Ltd, London, 2000

1

Originally published in Arabic as Al-Wala' wa'l-Bara' by Dar Taiba.

2000: First Edition

Typeset by Omar Ahmed & edited by Abu Ruqayyah.

ISBN 1 874263 809

Available from: and from

Al-Firdous Ltd.,   Ta-Ha Publishers Ltd.,
10 Fonthill Road   1 Wynne Road
London, N4 3HX   London SW9 0BB

Printed & Bound by Deluxe Printers, London
Tel : 020 8965 1771
Email : de-luxe@talk21.com

Table of Contents

4

INTRODUCTION: Prerequisites of the Doctrine of Alliance and Dissociation

We discussed in Section One the idea that the basis of alliance, in Islam, is love and that the basis of dissociation is anger. All actions in the world may be seen as either a confirmation or negation of this love; dissociation reaffirms your love, but its absence calls love's existence into question. Love, in fact, is a fundamental element in the world view of Islam. As Allah ﷻ has said,

> **Indeed, those who believe and do good works, the Most Beneficent (Allah) will bestow love for them.**[1]

And He ﷻ said,

> **Verily, my Lord is Most Merciful, Most Loving**[2]

> **And He is Oft-Forgiving, Full of Love**[3]

> **Those who believe are most resolute in their love for Allah**[4]

and finally, He ﷻ says:

---

[1] *Maryam*: 96.
[2] *Hud*: 90.
[3] *Al-Buruj*: 14.
[4] *Al-Baqarah*: 165.

Say, "If you really love Allah then follow me, Allah will love you.[5]

While the divine and the profane are clearly delimited, this does not prevent such and expression of love between Allah and his creatures. The link between Allah and His creation is one of mercy, of love and of trust. It is not, as the enemies of Islam have suggested, one founded upon blind fear, the threat of punishment and eternal damnation, Allah ﷻ has said,

Mighty is the word that comes out of their mouths. They utter nothing but a lie.[6]

The Love of Allah is a thing which no one may truly appreciate without first understanding something of the nature of Allah as described in the Qur'an and the Sunnah, and then feeling the presence of this nature in himself, in the depths of his own being. Likewise, the love, which you feel for Allah, is also a blessing, which no one can truly appreciate until it touches him. The Divine Love of Allah for any one of His creatures is then quite an extraordinary thing, supremely unmerited. In fact, the great blessing of Allah is that He guides His Creatures to His Love, and that He reveals to them its sweetness. [7]

Blessed again are the believing servants of Allah whom He has bound to one another in their love for Him,

---

[5] *Aal-Imran*: 31.
[6] *Al-Kahf*: 5.
[7] Sayyid Qutb, *"Adh-Dhilal"*, Vol.2/918-919.

it is the fresh clear water from which they all partake. Then Allah directed their love towards one another and caused it to bind them one to another, as the Prophet ﷺ has said, "A person is with whomever he loves".[8] Abdullah Ibn Masu'd ؓ said: "A man came to Allah's Apostle and said, 'O Allah's Apostle! What do you say about a man who loves some people but cannot catch up with their good deeds?' Allah's Apostle said, 'Everyone will be with those whom he loves." [9]

Anas ؓ said that a man once came to the Prophet ﷺ asking about the Hour. The Prophet ﷺ asked him: "What have you put forward for it?" He said, "I have not said many prayers, I have not fasted much nor given alms, but I love Allah and His Messenger". So he ﷺ told him, "You are with those whom you love". [10]

It should perhaps be pointed out here that this love is not to be understood as a kind of mystic or sublime power which can wipe out sin and iniquity, as some have mistakenly believed. Rather, it is a heartfelt love, which is translated into deeds. Allah ﷻ has said,

It shall not be in accordance with your desires (O Muslims), nor with those of the People of the Book. Whoever commits an evil deed shall

---

[8] "Sahih al-Bukhari", *Kitab al-Adab*, Vol.10/557, Hadith 6168.
[9] "Sahih al-Bukhari", *Kitab al-Adab*, Vol.10/557, Hadith 6169, and "Sahih Muslim", *Kitab al-Birr*, Vol.4/2034, Hadith 2640.
[10] "Sahih al-Bukhari", *Kitab al-Adab*, Vol.10/557, Hadith 6171, and "Sahih Muslim", *Kitab al-Birr*, Vol.4/2032, Hadith 2639.

have his recompense and shall find neither friend nor helper, to victory, except Allah.[11]

And He ﷻ said:

Say (O Muhammad to mankind): "If you love Allah then follow me, Allah will love you and forgive you your sins.   And Allah is Oft-Forgiving, Most Merciful".[12]

Al-Hassan said, "Don't be mislead into thinking that all is well when a person is to be with whom he loves, if the people he loves are still following the old ways. You will never be allowed to join the best of humanity, until you follow in their footsteps; follow their example and adopt their way of life; morning, evening and night you must live like them, strive to be one of them, to follow the road they have trod. For even though you may fall short in deeds, the heart of the matter is that you tried to do what was right. As for the Jews and the Christians and others like them, they loved their prophets but they would not support them; for they differed with them both in word and in deed, and chose for themselves some other path and so their destiny is the fire." [13]

---

[11] *An-Nisa'*: 123.
[12] *Aal-Imran*: 31.
[13] Ibn Rajab, p.133.

Love can be of four types: [14]

1. One Love is shared out among many different things. This, Allah describes in Surat *al-Baqarah*,

> **And of mankind are some who take (for worship) others besides Allah as rivals. They love them as they love Allah. But those who believe love Allah more. If only, those who do wrong could see, when they will see the torment, that all power belongs to Allah and that Allah is severe in punishment. When those who were followed, disown those who followed them, and they see the torment, then all their relations will be cut off from them. And those who followed will say "If only we had more chance to return (to the worldly life) we would disown them as they have disowned us. Thus Allah will show them the affliction of their own deeds and they shall not get out of the fire.[15]**

2. There is a perverse love of falsehood and of those who uphold it which has for its complement a hatred of truth and all who support it; this is a quality of hypocrisy.

3. There is a natural love; the attraction to wealth and the affection for children. There is nothing wrong in this, so long as it does not impinge upon obedience to Allah

---

[14] Muhammad Ibn Abdul Wahab, *Majmuat at-Tawhid*, p.17.
[15] *Al-Baqarah*: 165-167.

nor bring you into opposition to Him. This kind of love is permissible.

4. There is the love of those who defend the Right of Allah Alone and who revile disbelief. Love for them is the deepest bond of faith, and the supreme act of worship and devotion to one's Lord.

Since the love for the sake of Allah is the deepest bond of faith, as mentioned in the Hadith: "The strongest bond of Faith is the love for the sake of Allah and the hatred for the sake of Allah", the only way of achieving this bond and of allying yourself to Allah is by following the Shari'ah which Muhammad ﷺ brought to us. Other than this, there is no other means, so whoever follows some other path to this goal is a liar, just as the pagans who claim to draw near to Allah by worshipping something other than Him. Allah says,

> **We only worship them so that they will bring us even nearer to Allah**[16]

Similarly, He ﷻ said relating the claim of the Jews and the Christians,

> **We are the children of Allah and his most beloved**[17]

Yet all the while they adhere to their rejection of the authority of His Messengers, abandon their

---

[16] *Az-Zumar*: 3.
[17] *Al-Ma'idah*: 18.

obligations and immerse themselves in what has been forbidden to them, [18]

Once the Majesty of Allah fills the heart nothing else may then exist beside it, for the heart's complete devotion to Allah will not permit a love for anything but Allah, nor malice felt for the sake of anything but Allah. Whoever achieves this condition will be unable to act except in obedience to Allah. Sin rises out of love for those things reviled by Allah, or from a distaste for what is loved by Allah, it arises when the whims of the soul are given precedence to the love of Allah and awe of Him. [19]

Ibn Taymiyyah explains the enormity of this love saying, "There is in this world a paradise, whoever does not enter it shall not enter that of the world to come". Others have said, "Pity the people of the earth who have departed without ever tasting the best of what it contains. What is it that they have missed? It is the love of Allah, and of others for His sake, the longing for Him, the joyous reunion with Him, and the rejection of all who would challenge Him."[20]

As regards hatred for His sake, this is an essential prerequisite for loving Him. Similarly, the lover loves that which his beloved loves, and hates what is hated by the beloved. He supports whomever is supported by his beloved and the enemy of the beloved is his enemy. The

---

[18] Ibnu Rajab, "*Ja'mi' al-Ulum wal-Hikam*", p. 316.
[19] Ibnu Rajab, "*Ja'mi' al-Ulum wal-Hikam*", p. 320.
[20] "*Madarij as-Salikeen*", Vol.1/454.

pleasure of the beloved is also his pleasure, and so too is their anger shared. What his beloved requires he also requires, he forbids what his beloved forbids, for they are, in all things, agreed.

It is common knowledge that whoever loves Allah as he should must also bear hatred for His enemies, and that a part of their *Jihad* is to love what Allah loves. He ﷺ says:

Surely Allah loves those who fight in His cause in ranks as if they were a solid structure.[21]

Furthermore, Allah ﷻ has described those whom He loves and who love Him saying:

Humble towards the believers, hard towards the disbelievers [22]

That is to say that they deal with the believers with humility and compassion and take them under their wing, but the disbelievers may only expect severity, scorn, and derision. Allah ﷻ says:

Stern towards the disbelievers, merciful unto themselves.[23]

---

[21] *As-Saff*: 4.
[22] *Al-Ma'idah*: 54.
[23] *Al-Fath*: 29.

They fight in the Way of Allah, and never fear the blame of the blamers.[24]

The enemies of Allah are despised by the believers and are the eternal adversary in war,

Fight them, Allah will punish them by your hands and disgrace them and give you victory over them.[25]

The conclusion, of all this, is that the prerequisites of alliance and dissociation is that Muslims have rights upon one another.

---

[24] *Al-Ma'idah*: 54.
[25] *At-Tawbah*: 14.

CHAPTER ONE: The Rights of Muslims upon One Another

As we have already mentioned, love for the sake of Allah is the most profound bond which all Muslims share. From this bond the rights and obligations of Muslims with respect to one another are derived. These rights are many indeed, they include such things as; aid and assistance, affection, generosity and respect, justice and equality, and numerous other things, all of which are outlined both in the text of the Qur'an and in the Sunnah of the Prophet ﷺ. Of these rights the two most relevant to our discussion are assistance and affection.

1. Affection is meant to be between the believers. The disbelievers, the corrupt and the heretical have no place in it. Likewise, the Muslim wants for his brother what he wants for himself, as the Prophet ﷺ said, "None of you believes until he wants for his brother what he wants for himself."[26] (Agreed upon).

2. Assisting the Muslims is required by faith. Every Muslim is the brother of another regardless of race or colour, national origin or social class. You must help him and defend him with your money and your life. Whoever has refused to do this should take heed of the words of the Prophet ﷺ who said, "No (Muslim) man will desert a man who is a Muslim, in a place where his respect may be violated and his honour aspersed, without Allah

---

[26] "Sahih al-Bukhari", *Kitab al-Iman*, Vol.1/57, Hadith 13, and "Sahih Muslim", *Kitab al-Iman*, Vol.1/67, Hadith 45.

deserting him in a place where he wishes his help; and no (Muslim) man who will help a Muslim, in a place where his honour may be aspersed and his respect violated, without Allah helping him in a place where he wishes his help"[27].

Allah ﷻ himself praised the *Ansar* for their assistance to their brothers from Makkah saying:

Those who believe and who migrated and who struggled in the Path of Allah, and those who gave shelter and aid, these are the true believers.[28]

The Prophet ﷺ also ordered the believers to be mindful to assist one another saying, "Help your brother, whether he is an oppressor or he is an oppressed one"[29]. Helping him, when he is right, goes without saying; to help him when he is wrong means to prevent him from oppressing others. He ﷺ also said, "A Muslim is a brother of another Muslim, he should not oppress him, nor should he hand him over to an oppressor. Whoever fulfilled the needs of his brother, Allah will fulfil his needs; whoever brought his (Muslim) brother out of a discomfort, Allah will bring him out of the discomforts of the Day of Resurrection, and whoever screened a

---

[27] Abu Dawud, *Kitab al-Adab*, Vol.5/197, Hadith 4884, and *Musnad* Ahmad, Vol.4/30. Albani classifies it as Hadith *Hasan*, See: *"Sahih al-Ja'mi' as-Sagheer"*, Vol.5/160, Hadith 5566.
[28] *Al-Anfa'l*: 74.
[29] "Sahih al-Bukhari", *Kitab al-Madhalim*, Vol.5/98, Hadith 2443.

Muslim, Allah will screen him on the Day of Resurrection."[30]

Within Islamic society every individual is important. If any one's rights are abused, then everyone is damaged; they are like the parts of a body; if some part of it is ill, all of it is ill. Thus the Prophet ﷺ said, "A believer to another believer is like a building whose different parts enforce each other"[31], and he ﷺ said, "You see the believers as regard their being merciful among themselves, showing love among themselves and being kind among themselves, resembling one body; so that, if any part of the body is not well, then the whole body shares the sleeplessness and fever with it." (reference reported previously). Also he ﷺ said, "The believer is the reflection of his brother; and the believer is another believer's brother, who guards him against loss and protects him when he is absent."[32]

If we were to report all the relevant sources here our discussion would lengthen considerably. Suffice it to say that the conduct of the Prophet ﷺ, the Companions and those who followed in their footsteps and guidance, throughout the history of the Islamic society, only confirms this important principle. The cohesion and

---

[30] "Sahih al-Bukhari", *Kitab al-Madhalim*, Vol.5/97, Hadith 2442, and "Sahih Muslim", *Kitab al-Birr was-Silah*, Vol.4/1996, Hadith 2580.
[31] "Sahih al-Bukhari", *Kitab al-Adab*, Vol.10/442, Hadith 6026, "Sahih Muslim", *Kitab al-Birr was-Silah*, Vol.4/1999, Hadith 2585.
[32] Al-Bukhari, "*al-Adab al-Mufrad*", p.70, Abu Dawud, *Kitab al-Adab*, Vol.5/217, Hadith 4918, this Hadith is classified as *Hasan*, See: "*Sahih al-Ja'mi' as-Sagheer*", Vol.6/6, Hadith 6532.

solidarity of the Muslims has been exemplary, whether on the communal or individual level; whenever the alliances and the enmities of the Muslims have been, clearly, for the sake of Allah. The Muslims will never be successful except if they observe this fundamental truth; that the Muslim's love for his brother is like his love for his own self; that he feels his pain as if it were his own; that he is pleased by his success as if it were his own accomplishment. Finally, Allah will surely come to the aid of the one who is mindful to serve Him.

As for helping the Muslims, this includes such things as coming actively to their defence, giving them whatever material and moral support is necessary whenever they are threatened, offering their wealth and their lives to break the power of the oppressor. They would reject all those who long for the humiliation of the Muslims. They concern themselves with the affairs of the Muslims wherever they are, helping and supporting them as much as they can.

All of these things serve to cement relations between Muslims, bringing them together in word and deed, in the fold of Islam.

CHAPTER TWO: Migration

This is one of the most important facets of our discussion, since alliance and dissociation are always among the primary motivating factors of migration for the sake of Allah. We will divide our discussion of this into two broad areas:

1. Living among the disbelievers and its ruling.
2. Migrating from the abode of disbelief to the abode of Islam.

1. Living in the abode of disbelief

The jurists have explained the complimentary concepts of the "Abode of Disbelief" and that of "Islam" as follows:

The Abode of Disbelief is whatever land is ruled by the disbelievers, in which the laws of the disbelievers are supreme and political power is in their hands. These lands may be of two types. One which is at war with the Muslims and one which enjoys a truce with them. The determining factor is that it is ruled by the laws of the disbelievers; for it is the "Abode of Disbelief" or "*Dar ul-Kufr*", even if a large majority of Muslims live there.[33]

---

[33] Abdur Rahman Ibn Sa'dee, "*Al-Fatawee as-Sa'diyya*", Vol.1/92, 1st Edition, 1388 A.H., Dar al-Hayat, Damascus.

The Abode of Islam is any land that is ruled by the Muslims, where the Shari'ah is the supreme law and the Muslims hold political power. It is *Dar ul-Islam*, even if the majority of the population are disbelievers, so long as the Muslims rule it according to the Shari'ah.[34]

As Islam is the religion of dignity and authority, it was impossible to think of any Muslim submitting himself to the disbelievers; indeed it is forbidden for a Muslim to go to live amongst them and acknowledge their authority over him, because his presence amongst them would make him feel weak and isolated, and, then he would become docile and apologetic before them. He would first be called upon to approve of them, and then to follow them. But Muslims should be filled with morale and confidence, they should be leaders, not followers. They should hold the reins of power; no power should be above them but that of Allah. Therefore Muslims were forbidden to remain in countries where Islam is of no account, except when they are able to freely practice their religion and to observe it without any impediment, and without any fear that their presence there could damage them in any way. If this is not the case, then they must migrate to a better place where the authority of Islam is of some account. If they refuse to do so, while they are able, then they would have no further claims on this religion. About this Allah has spoken in Surat *an-Nisa'*:

> **Verily! As for those whom the Angels have taken (in death) while they are wronging themselves (as they stayed among the**

---

[34] Ibid. Vol.1/92.

disbelievers even though emigration was obligatory to them), they (angels) asked them, "In what condition were you?". They replied, "We were weak and oppressed on earth". The Angels asked, "Was not the earth of Allah spacious enough for you to migrate therein?" Such men will find their abode in Hell - what an evil destination! Except the weak ones among men, women and children who were unable to devise a plan, nor are they able to direct their way [35]

The Prophet ﷺ said, "I am not responsible for any Muslim who stays among polytheists. They asked: 'Why, Apostle of Allah?' He said: 'Their fires should not be visible to one another.', and he ﷺ said, "Who joins the polytheists and lives with them then he is like them" and he ﷺ said: "Migration will not end until repentance ends, and repentance will not end until the sun rises in the west." [36]

Al-Hassan Ibn Salih said: "whoever remains in the land of the enemy, will be treated like the disbelievers, so long as he was able to join the Muslims but did not do it. If one of the disbelievers accepts Islam, but still remains with the disbelievers, even though he was able to go to join the Muslims, he is to be treated like

---

[35] *An-Nisa'*: 97-98.
[36] *"Al-Musnad"*, Vol.4/99, Abu Dawud, *Kitab al-Jihad*, Vol.3/7, Hadith 2479, and ad-Darami, *Kitab as-Siyyar*, Vol.2/239. Albani classifies it as *Sahih*. See: *"Sahih al-Ja'mi' as-Sagheer"*, Vol.6/186, Hadith 7346.

them; neither his blood nor his property will be protected." [37]

Al-Hassan said: "If a Muslim emigrates to the land of the disbelievers, yet does not renounce Islam, he will be an apostate by virtue of his abandonment of *'Dar ul-Islam'*"[38]. (The Arabic text of the preceding passage refers to the land of the disbelievers as *'dar ul-harb'* and *'Ard ul-Adu'*, that is: the 'land of the enemy'; this indicates an active military opposition to the Muslims, as if in a state of war).

Ibn Hazm states that: "Whoever joins the 'land of war and disbelief', of his own free will and in defiance of whoever amongst the Muslims calls him to his side, is by virtue of this act an apostate, by all the laws of apostasy, in Islam. Whoever is able to kill him must do so. His property is unprotected, his marriage null and void, all his rights are swept away.

But whoever flees to the 'land of war' for fear of oppression, who neither opposes the Muslims in anything nor bears any malice towards them, and who was not able to find any refuge among the Muslims, is free of any guilt since he was compelled to leave.

As for someone who takes the Muslims as his enemies, offering his help and his service to the disbelievers, he is a disbeliever. But those who would emigrate to non-Muslim lands in search of wealth or

---

[37] Al-Jasaas, *"Ahkam al-Qur'an"*, Vol.3/216.
[38] Ibd.

prosperity to live under their protection, while they were able to go to live amongst the Muslims in their own land, but still do not withdraw themselves from the disbelievers; such people are not far from the fold of disbelief, and we can find no possible excuse for them, so we ask Allah's Forgiveness.

As for the person who lives in the land of *Karmathians* by his own free will, he is without doubt a disbeliever, because they are avowed enemies of Islam, disbelievers and apostates who only long for the destruction of the Muslims. Concerning those who live in a land where some heretic tendencies, leading to disbelief, are manifested, they are not considered disbelievers, as Islam is supreme in the land where it is possible to practice Islam openly; to confirm the message of the Prophet Muhammad ﷺ, read the Qur'an, establish the prayer, perform the fast of Ramadan and fulfil one's obligations entirely.

The words of the Prophet ﷺ, "I am not responsible for any Muslim who stays among polytheists" should clarify what we have said so far. It is clear that the Prophet ﷺ refers here to the '*Dar ul-Harb*', and because he ﷺ appointed some Companions as governors of Khaibar (Jewish land), even though everyone who lived there were Jews.

If a disbeliever conquers a Muslim country, then acknowledges their religion (Islam), but assumes authority over them, and then claims any other religion than Islam, whoever lives with him, supports, or serves him in any way is a disbeliever, even if he claims to be a Muslim, as aforementioned."[39]

Sheikh Hamad Ibn Ateeq, may Allah have mercy upon him, divided those Muslims who live in non-Islamic countries into three groups: Those who prefer to live amongst Non-Muslims because of their affection for them; those who live amongst non-Muslims yet ignore their obligation to denounce disbelief; and those who live amongst the non-Muslims but uphold their obligation to denounce disbelief.

The first group: stays amongst the disbelievers by choice and inclination, they praise and commend them, and are happy to disassociate themselves from the Muslims. They help the disbelievers in their struggle against the Muslims in any way they can, physically, morally, and financially. Such people are disbelievers, their position is actively and deliberately opposed to religion. Allah says,

The believers shall not take the disbelievers as allies in preference to the believers. Whoever does this shall never be helped by Allah in any way [40]

At-Tabari remarks that such a person would have washed his hands of Allah, and that Allah would have nothing to do with a person who actively rejects Him and denies His Religion. Allah ﷻ says:

---

[39] Ibn Hazm, *al-Muhalla'*: Vol.13/139-140.
[40] *Aal-Imran*: 28.

O you who believe! Do not take the Jews and the Christians as protectors, they are protectors of one another, whoever takes them as protectors is one of them.[41]

Then, in the words of the Prophet ﷺ: "Whoever joins the disbelievers and lives amongst them is one of them"[42].

Abdullah Ibn Omar said: "Whoever settles amongst the disbelievers, celebrates their feasts and joins in their revelry and dies in their midst will likewise be raised to stand with them on the Day of Resurrection."[43].

Muhammad Ibn Abdul Wahhab, may Allah have mercy upon him, mentioned that in the case of a Muslim whose people remained bound to disbelief and followed the enemies of Islam, he too would become a disbeliever if he refused to abandon his people, just because he found it difficult. He would end up fighting against the Muslims alongside his nation, with his money and life. And if they were to order him to marry his father's wife, but could not prevent that unless he migrates from his country, he would be forced to marry her. His alliance and participation with them in their campaign against Islam and their struggle against Allah and His Messenger is far worse than marrying his father's wife. He is also a disbeliever, about whom Allah has said:

---

[41] *Al-Ma'idah*: 51.
[42] Ibn Ateeq, *"Ad-Difaa'"*, p,10-12.
[43] Ibn Taymiyyah said in his book: *"Iqtidha' as-Sirat al-Mustaqeem"*, p.200, that the chain of narration of this Hadith is Sahih.

You will find others who hope for your protection, and for that of their own people. But whenever they are sent to temptation, they yield thereto. If they do not withdraw from you, nor offer you peace, nor restrain their hands, then seize them and kill them wherever you may find them. In their case, We have given you a clear warrant against them.[44]

The second group: are those who remain amongst the disbelievers because of money, family or homeland. He does not demonstrate a strong attachment to his religion (Islam), nor does he emigrate. He does not support the disbelievers against the Muslims, whether in word or deed. His heart is not bound to them, nor does he speak on their behalf. Such a person is not considered a disbeliever merely because he continues to live among the disbelievers, but many would say that he has disobeyed Allah and His Messenger by not going to live among the Muslims, even though he may secretly hate the disbelievers. Allah has said,

Verily! As for those whom the Angels have taken (in death) while they are wronging themselves (as they stayed among the disbelievers even though emigration was obligatory to them), they (angels) asked them, "In what condition were you?". They replied, "We were weak and oppressed on earth". The Angels asked, "Was not the earth of Allah spacious enough for you to migrate therein?"

---

[44] *An-Nisa'*: 91.

25

Such men will find their abode in Hell - what an evil destination!"[45]

Ibn Kathir remarks: They were ⟨**wronging themselves**⟩ by refusing to emigrate. He continues by saying that this verse establishes a general rule which applies to anyone who is prevented from practising his religion, yet willingly remains among the disbelievers. There is no disagreement among the scholars, and the sources all state that this course of action is prohibited. [46]

Al-Bukhari relates that Ibn Abbas ﷺ said that this verse was about "Some people from among the Muslims who stayed with the Pagans of Makkah, swelling their ranks, in the days of the Prophet ﷺ. When fighting broke out some of them were killed and some wounded. Then Allah revealed the verse:

⟨**Verily! As for those whom the Angels have taken (in death) while they are wronging themselves**⟩"[47].

Whatever excuses they may have offered were rejected by the revelation,

Say, 'If your fathers, your sons, your brothers, your wives, your kinsmen, the wealth which you have acquired, the commerce in which you fear a decline, or the houses you love - if these are dearer to you than Allah and His

---

[45] *An-Nisa'*: 97.
[46] "Tafsir Ibn Kathir", 2/343, and Ibn Ateeq, *"Ad-Difaa'"*, p.13.
[47] *"Sahih al-Bukhari"*, Vol.8/262, Hadith 4596.

Messenger, and striving hard and fighting in His cause, then wait until Allah brings about His Decision (Torment). Allah does not guide those who are *Al-Faasiqun*.[48]

Anyone who refuses to emigrate uses one of these eight excuses. But these excuses have already been rejected by Allah, Who has said that those who make such claims are disobedient to Him, and this was specifically with regard to those who chose to remain in Makkah which is the holiest place on earth. Allah required the believers to quit this place, and even love for it was not an acceptable excuse for refusal. How would such an excuse fare then for places other than Makkah? [49]

The third group: are those who may remain among the disbelievers without impediment, and they are two categories:

1. Those who are openly able to proclaim their religion and dissociate themselves from disbelief. When they are able, they clearly disassociate themselves from the disbelievers and tell them openly that they are far from truth, and that they are wrong. This is what is known as '*Izhar ad-Din*' or 'assertion of Islam'. This is what exonerates a person from the obligation to emigrate. As Allah has said: **《Say, "O Disbelievers, I do not worship what you worship and you are not worshipers of what I worship.. 》.**

---

[48] *Al-Ma'idah*: 24.
[49] Ibn Ateeq, "*Ad-Difaa'*", p.13-14, and see also, Ibn Ateeq's "*Bayan an-Najaat wal Fakak*", p.70-72.

27

Thus, Muhammad ﷺ was commanded to tell the disbelievers of their clear disbelief and that their religion was not the same, nor was their worship, nor what they worshipped. That they could not be in the service of Allah, so long as they remained in the service of falsehood. He was commanded to express his satisfaction with Islam as his religion and his denial of the faith of the disbelievers. Allah ﷻ says:

Say (O Muhammad): "O mankind! If you are in doubt about my religion (Islam), then know that I do not worship what you worship besides Allah, rather I worship Allah Who causes you to die, and I am commanded to be among the believers. And (it is inspired to me): Direct your face (O Muhammad) towards the religion *Hanifan* (Islamic Monotheism), and never be one of the *Mushrikeen*. [50]

Therefore, Whoever does this is not obliged to emigrate.

Asserting one's religion does not mean that you simply leave people to worship whatever they please without comment, like the Christians and the Jews do. It means that you must clearly and plainly disapprove of what they worship, and show enmity towards the disbelievers; failing this there is no assertion of Islam.

2. Those who live amongst the disbelievers, and have not the means to leave nor the strength to assert themselves, have a license to remain. Allah ﷻ says,

---

[50] *Yunus*: 104-105.

Except for the weak ones among men, women and children who are unable to devise a plan, nor to direct their way.[51]

But the exemption comes after a promise to those who remain among the disbelievers, that,

Such men will find their abode in Hell - What an evil destination![52]

It is an exemption to those who could not devise a plan nor find any other way out. Ibn Kathir remarks: "These were people who could not rid themselves of the disbelievers, and even had they been able to do so, they would not have been able to direct their way"[53].

Allah says:

And what is wrong with you that you fight not in the Cause of Allah, and for those weak, ill-treated and oppressed among men, women, and children, whose cry is: "Our Lord! Rescue us from this town whose people are oppressors; and raise for us from You one who will protect, and raise for us from You one who will help"[54].

---

[51] *An-Nisa'*: 98.
[52] *An-Nisa'*: 97.
[53] *"Tafsir Ibn Kathir"*, Vol.2/343.
[54] *An-Nisa'*: 75.

So in the first verse, Allah ﷻ mentions their situation, their weakness and inability to find any way to extricate themselves, and in the second, He ﷻ mentions their plea to Allah to deliver them from their oppressors and to give them a protector, a helper and guide to victory. For these people Allah ﷻ says:

For these there is hope that Allah will forgive them, and Allah is Ever Oft-Pardoning, Oft-Forgiving.[55]

Al-Baghawi commented that: "A Muslim who becomes a captive of the disbelievers must flee, if he is able, as he would not be permitted to remain under them. If they make him give his word that he would not run away if they were to release him, he should give them his word, but then he must try to escape; there would be no guilt upon him for his lie, since they had obligated him themselves. But if he had given them his promise, in order to ingratiate them to himself, he would be obliged to escape, just the same, but must also offer penance for his wilful deception of their trust"[56].

The rulings about travel to disbelieving countries (*Dar ul-Harb*) for purposes of trade are broadly detailed. If you are able to assert your faith, while not supporting the disbelievers, then this is permitted. Indeed, some of the Companions of the Prophet ﷺ travelled to some countries of disbelievers in search of trade, among them Abu Bakr as-Siddiq. The Prophet ﷺ did not prevent them

---

[55] *An-Nisa'*: 99.
[56] Al-Baghawi, *"Sharh as-Sunnah"*, Vol.10/246.

from this, as Imam Ahmad points out in his *Musnad* and elsewhere.[57]

If you are unable to assert your religion or avoid supporting them, then it is not permitted to venture amongst them for trading purposes. The subject has been addressed by the scholars and the relevant support for their position will be found in the Prophet's *Ahaadeeth*. Allah has required all believers to uphold their faith and to oppose the disbelievers. Nothing is allowed to undermine or interfere with these obligations.[58]

While this is quite clear from many different sources, we still find a carefree attitude among many Muslims today with regard to this subject. The forming of friendships with those who are rightly our enemies, and establishing communities in their countries has been trivialised. Remarkably, some Muslims even send their children to the West to study Islamic Law and Arabic in European and American universities! This will stand as an absurd monument to the foolishness of those Muslims of the twentieth century, who sent their children to the disbelievers to study Islamic Law and Arabic!

Our scholars have warned us enough of the dangers which these questions raise, and they have carefully explained the perils of such educational exchanges, and of the desire of the disbelievers to corrupt

---

[57] This is quoted from the *"al-Jami' al-Farid"*, but the author was unable to find any such reference in the *Musnad*.

[58] See: *"al-Jami' al-Farid"*, p.382, 2nd Edition.

the minds of our youth to turn them away from Islam, so we should take time to consider what we are doing.[59]

2. Emigration from the Abode of Disbelief to Muslim Countries

"Hijrah" is the Arabic word for emigration. It means, ultimately, to separate or abandon. In religious terminology it means to move from a non-Muslim place of abode to a place where there is a presence of Islam[60]. It is a fact that those whose religion is Islam; which is based on directing all kinds of worship to Allah, rejecting and showing hatred to polytheism and disbelievers; will never be left at peace by the antithesis of Islam, as Allah has said:

They will not stop fighting you until they turn you away from your religion, if they are able [61]

and He ﷻ says about the people of the Cave:

For if they come to know of you, they will stone you or turn you back to their religion, then you will never prosper [62]

---

[59] Two of these scholars are Muhammad Muhammad Hussein in his valuable books: *"Al-Ittijaahaat al-Wataniyyah"*, *"Al-Islam wal Hadaara al-Gharbiyya"* and *"Husununa Muhaddada min Dakhilihaa"*; also there is a valuable study by Sheikh Muhammad Lutfi as-Sabaagh called *"Al-Ibtia'th wa Makhaatiruhu"*.

[60] *"Fath al-Bari"*, Vol.1/16.

[61] *Al-Baqarah*: 217.

and finally, about the disbelievers declared aim, Allah ﷻ says:

Those who disbelieved said to their Messengers: "We will drive you out of our lands, or you shall return you to our religion". So their Lord revealed this to them: "Surely We shall destroy the *Zaalimun* (disbelievers)"[63]

Likewise, Waraqah Ibn Nawfal said, anticipating the mission of the Prophet ﷺ: "I wish I could be young at the time when you will be driven away by your people." He said, "Will they throw me out?". "Yes, Nawfal replied, no one has ever come with a thing such as this who was not then driven away by his own people". So it was that the Quraish first drove the Prophet ﷺ from Makkah to Ta'if, then to Madinah; and some of his Companions emigrated twice to Abyssinia.[64]

The *Hijrah* is a vitally important aspect of Islam; it is at once the guiding principle of alliance and dissociation and the supreme example of it. The Muslims could never have abandoned their homes and families, exposing themselves to the pain of separation and the hardship of migration if it had not been indispensable to the practice of their religion and the assertion of Islam in the land. Allah promised these emigrants a great reward in this world and the next, saying:

---

[62] *Al-Kahf*: 20.
[63] *Ibrahim*: 13.
[64] Ibnu Ateeq, *"ad-Difaa'"*, pp.18, 19, and *"Seerat Ibn Hisham"*, Vol.1, p.254.

> **Those who left their homes for the sake of Allah after having suffered persecution shall be settled in comfort in this world but in the next is the greater reward if they but knew. Those who were steadfast and who upon their Lord totally depend.**[65]

Hijrah has a comprehensive meaning as understood in Islam. It is not simply just the act of moving from one place to another; from a non-Muslim country to a Muslim country. Ibn al-Qayyim explains that it is, in fact, an emigration of the body and the spirit. A physical movement from one place to another and a spiritual migration to Allah and His Messenger ﷺ. It is this second migration which constitutes the real migration, as the body simply follows the soul. Thus, the meaning of moving from one thing to something else is that the heart moves from the love of something other than Allah to love of Allah; from servitude of something or other to the service and worship of Allah; from fear of something or other to hope in and reliance upon Allah. It is Allah Who is the object of one's hope and fear; prayers are addressed to Him; and He is the One before Whom one feels humility and awe. This is the meaning of flight which Allah mentions in the command: ❰**So flee to Allah**❱. [66]

This is the essence of monotheism (*Tawhid*); that you abandon all else and flee to Allah. Flight is from something to something else, and in this case it is from

---

[65] *An-Nahl*: 41-42.
[66] *Az-Zariyat*: 50.

whatever is odious in the sight of Allah ﷻ to whatever He loves. This is essentially an expression of either love or revulsion. Whoever flees a thing exchanges an undesirable thing for something better, in response to his own preference. This kind of migration may be more or less strongly motivated depending upon the degree of love in one's heart. The stronger or deeper the love, the more complete and secure is the migration. If this love is shallow then the migration is less secure, and this may continue to the point of complete indifference.[67]

The rulings regarding actual physical migration from the lands of the disbelievers to a land of Islam is as follows:

Imam al-Khattabee[68] points out that in the early days of Islam physical migration was recommended but not required, as Allah ﷻ says:

Whoever migrates for the sake of Allah will find refuge and great bounty in the earth.[69]

---

[67] Ibn al-Qayyim, "*Ar-Risaalat at-Tabuqiyyah*" , pp.14-18, 2nd edition, 1394, Egypt.

[68] His full name is Imam Hamad Ibn Muhammad Ibn Ibrahim Ibn al-Khattab, of the descendants of Zayd Ibn al-Khattab, he is known as Abu Sulayman. He was a jurist, narrator of Hadith, a poet, and a linguist. Among his students, al-Hakim an-Nisaaburi. Al-Khattabee was born in Kabul in 319 A.H. and died in 388 A.H. For more information, see: the introduction of "*Maalim as-Sunan*" published with "*Sunan Abu Dawud*", Vol.1/11, and az-Zarkali's "*Al-A'laam*", Vol.2/273, 4th edition.

[69] *An-Nisa'*: 100.

This was revealed when the pagan persecution of the Muslims at Makkah was on the rise, after the Prophet ﷺ has left for Madinah. But after this they were subsequently commanded to follow him there in order to be with him. They were required to co-operate as a single community, to learn their religion from the Prophet ﷺ and to get an understanding of it directly from him. At this time the greatest threat to the Muslim community was posed by the Quraish, who were the masters of Makkah. After Makkah fell, the obligation was again lifted and migration became once again a matter of preference. Bearing this in mind, we are in a better position to understand the report of Muawiyah who related that the Prophet ﷺ said: "Migration will not end until repentance ends, and repentance will not end until the sun rises in the west". And that of Ibn Abbas who said: "The Prophet ﷺ said, on the day of the conquest of Makkah, 'There is no migration (after the conquest), except for *Jihad* and good intentions, and when you are called for *Jihad*, you should immediately respond to the call"[70]. The chain of narrators in Ibn Abbas's Hadith is Sahih, but that of Muawiyah is disputed by some.[71]

Because of the significance of the *Hijrah*, especially in the early days of Islam, Allah ﷻ severed the ties of mutual support between the Muslims who

---

[70] "*Sahih al-Bukhari*", *The Book of Jihad*, Vol.6/37, hadith 2825.
[71] Al-Khattabee, "*Maalim as-Sunan*", Vol.3/352, revised by Ahmad Shakir and Muhammad Haamid al-Faqee, see also: "*An-Naasikh wal Mansukh*", p.207.

migrated to Madinah and those who chose to remain in Makkah, saying:

> **Indeed those who believe and who migrated and who struggle in the Path of Allah with their wealth and their lives, and those who gave them shelter and who gave them help, these are allies of one another. But those who believe yet did not migrate have no part in this alliance until they too migrate. If they seek your assistance in faith you must help them except against a people with whom you have a treaty. Allah is well aware of what you do** [72]

Following this, Allah 🕮 praises the migrants and the Helpers (*Muhajirun* and *Ansar*) saying:

> **Those who believe and who migrated and who struggled in the Path of Allah, and those who gave shelter and aid, these are the true believers. Forgiveness and bountiful provision are theirs.** [73]

We have already discussed the *Muhajirin* and the *Ansar*; what we will look at now are those believers who did not make the *Hijrah*, but who stayed in Makkah during the time of conflict. Allah 🕮 says:

> **Verily! As for those whom the angels take (in death) while they are wronging themselves (as**

---

[72] *Al-Anfal*: 72.
[73] *Al-Anfal*: 74.

they stayed among the disbelievers even though emigration was obligatory for them), they (angels) say to them: "In what condition were you?" They reply: "We were weak and oppressed on earth". The angels say: "Was not the earth spacious enough for you to emigrate therein?" Such men will find their abode in Hell - What an evil destination. Except for the weak ones among men, women and children who are unable to devise a plan, nor to direct their way. For these there is hope that Allah will forgive them, and Allah is Ever Oft Pardoning, Oft-Forgiving. [74]

Al-Bukhari relates that Ibn Abbas said that some Muslims used to live among the disbelievers, increasing their population during the Prophet ﷺ era. They were killed or injured in the fighting, so Allah ﷻ revealed: ❮Verily! As for those whom the angels take (in death) while they are wronging themselves❯.

Therefore, the believers who did not emigrate but who remained in their homes had no share in the war booty, nor in its fifth part, except in the battles in which they took part, as Imam Ahmad has stated[75]. This is indicated by a Hadith mentioned by Imam Ahmad and also reported by Muslim on the authority of Sulaiman Ibn Buraida, on the authority of his father, that: "Whenever the Prophet ﷺ appointed a commander over an army or a detachment, he advised him privately to be mindful of his

---

[74] *An-Nisa'*: 97-99.
[75] *"Tafsir Ibn Kathir"*, Vol.4/40.

duty to Allah ﷻ and to guard the welfare of the Muslims who were under his command. Then, he said, "Fight in the name of Allah, and for His Sake. Fight whoever disbelieves in Allah. Do not embezzle the spoils, nor break your pledge, nor mutilate the dead bodies, nor kill children. When you meet your enemies, the polytheists, invite them to three things and if they make a positive response to you, accept it and withhold yourselves from doing any harm to them. Then invite them to migrate from their lands to the land of the Emigrants and tell them that if they will do so, they will have (all the privileges and obligations) that the Emigrants have; but if they refuse to migrate, tell them that they will be like the Bedouin Muslims and will be subjected to the Commands of Allah ﷻ which are applicable to other Muslims and they will not be entitled to any booty nor *Fai'* unless they perform *Jihad* along with the Muslims. If they should refuse, demand *Jizyah* from them; but if they agree to pay *Jizyah*, accept it from them and restrain your hands from them. But if they refuse to pay *Jizyah*, seek Allah's Succour and fight against them..."[76].

The preceding discussion about *Hijrah* may be summarised as follows:

1. Migration from the lands of disbelievers to the lands of Muslims was mandatory in the time of the Prophet ﷺ, and it is still obligatory till the Day of Judgement. The obligation which the Prophet ﷺ lifted after the conquest of Makkah was that of taking up residence near him.

---

[76] "*Musnad* Ahmad", Vol.5/352, and "Sahih Muslim", "*The Book of Jihad*", Vol.3/1357, Hadith, 1731.

Whoever accepts Islam while living among those who are at war with Muslims must leave to make his home among the Muslims.[77]

This is supported by the Hadith of Mujaashi' Ibn Mas'ud who said: "I took my brother to the Prophet ﷺ, after the Conquest of Makkah, and said, "O Allah's Apostle! I have come to you with my brother so that you may take a pledge of allegiance from him for migration." The Prophet ﷺ said, "The people of migration (i.e. those who migrated to Madinah before the Conquest) enjoyed the privileges of migration (i.e. there is no need for migration anymore))." I said to the Prophet ﷺ, "For what will you take his pledge of allegiance?" The Prophet ﷺ said, "I will take his pledge of allegiance for Islam, Belief, and for *Jihad*"[78].

2. It is obligatory to leave the lands of the *Bidah* (innovation). Imam Malik said: "None of you may remain in a country where the Companions are cursed"[79].

3. It is obligatory to leave a place where forbidden practices are rife since it is mandatory for Muslims to demand observance of the Law[80]. In this regard, Ibn Taymiyyah said, "The state of a place reflects the state of a person. It is possible to be sometimes a Muslim and at other times a disbeliever; sometimes sincere and at other

[77] Ibn al-Arabi, "*Ahkaam al-Qur'an*", Vol.1/484, and an-Nawawi's "*Sharh Muslim*", Vol.13/8, and "*Tafsir al-Qurtubi*" Vol.5/308.
[78] "*Sahih Al-Bukhari*", "The Book of *Jihad*", 6/189, Hadith 3079.
[79] Ibn al-Arabi, "*Ahkaam al-Qur'an*", Vol.1/484-485.
[80] Ibn al-Arabi, "*Ahkaam al-Qur'an*", Vol.1/484-485.

times hypocritical; sometimes good and pious and at other times rotten and corrupt. Thus, a person becomes like the place of his abode. The migration of a person from a land of disbelief and profanity to one of faith and probity is an expression of repentance and of his turning away from disobedience and perversion to belief and obedience. This is so until the Day of Resurrection." [81]

4. One must flee persecution and oppression. This is to be counted as one of the many blessings of Allah ﷻ that he has given His license, to whoever fears for himself and his own safety, to go and find some sanctuary for himself. The first to do this was Abraham ﷺ who, when he was threatened by his own people said: **❴I will emigrate for the sake of my Lord❵**, (29:26), and, **❴I am going to my Lord, He shall guide me❵**, (37:99). Then there was Moses: **❴So he escaped from there, vigilant and fearing for his life, and said "My Lord deliver me from these oppressors"❵**, (28:21). [82]

5. In times of epidemic, people were required to leave the city and remain in the hinterland until the threat of disease had passed. The exception to this is in times of plague.[83]

---

[81] *"Majmu' al-Fatawa"*, 18/284.

[82] Ibn al-Arabi, *"Ahkaam al-Qur'an"*, Vol.1/485.

[83] "Sahih al-Bukhari", *"The Book of at-Tib"*, Vol.10/142, Hadith 5686, and "Sahih Muslim", *The Book of al-Qisama"*, Vol.3/1296, Hadith 1271. For the Hadith of plague, see: "Sahih al-Bukhari", *"The Book of at-Tib"*, Vol.10/179, Hadith 5728, and Muslim *"The Book of as-Salam"*, Vol.4/1741, Hadith 2219.

6. If one fears for the safety of his family or the security of his property then he must also flee since security of one's possessions is like the safety of one's person.[84]

Finally, migration, like anything else, is in the first instance a matter of intention, for the Prophet ﷺ said: "Indeed actions are but by intention, and each will be rewarded according to his intent. So whose goal is to migrate for Allah and His Messenger, his migration is for Allah and His Messenger, and whose aim is to migrate to some worldly gain or to take the hand of a woman in marriage, his migration is to that which he has sought."[85]

---

[84] Ibn al-Arabi, "Ahkaam al-Qur'an", Vol.1/486.
[85] "Sahih al-Bukhari", "The Book of Bad' al-Wahy", Vol.1/9, Hadith 1, and "Sahih Muslim", "The Book of al-Imaara", Vol.3/1515, Hadith 1907.

CHAPTER THREE: *Jihad* for Allah's Sake

This is one of the most important aspects of alliance and dissociation in Islam, it separates truth from falsehood, it separates the forces of Allah from those of Satan. The fundamental meaning of the word "*Jihad*" in Arabic is "hardship" or "struggle". In religious terminology this means to struggle against disbelievers.[1] It can also imply struggle against Satan, against corruption and against the darkness of one's own soul.

The darkness of one's soul is dispelled by the light of religious knowledge, by learning and then to applying what one has learnt to one's own life, and after this by teaching it to others. The struggle against Satan is in the fight against doubt, when it casts its shadow over the heart and entices one to join the glittering illusion of the treacherous, rejected Pretender. So, the struggle against the disbelievers is to be conducted with body and soul, wealth, tongue and heart; with all one's force and might against the powers of darkness and oppression. The struggle against corruption is a physical challenge raised in the face of falsehood; but if one cannot do this, be in open denunciation of it; but if one cannot even do this, let there be a willingness to struggle within one's heart.[2]

We have already discussed the nature of the powers of Satan and of the forces of Allah; how the

---

[1] Ibn Hajar, "*Fath al-Ba'ree*", Vol.6/3.
[2] Ibn Hajar, "*Fath al-Ba'ree*", Vol.6/3.

divisions between them are fundamental, and how they shall remain until the coming of the Hour. This is because the two have goals which are diametrically opposed and mutually exclusive. There is no common ground between them. The forces of Allah will strive for the establishment of the Shari'ah in its totality. The forces of evil will never tolerate this and will spare no expense to prevent it, so long as they are able.

We also discussed dissociation saying that the highest expression of it is *Jihad* for the Sake of Allah, because it is the only way to sever truth from falsehood; to sever the Party of Allah and the party of Satan.

Going back to the conduct of the Prophet's ﷺ life, we find that *Jihad* became a normality soon after his migration. This stands as proof of the importance of *Jihad* and of the establishment of this faith. It is in the total consecration of one's being to the struggle for Allah's Cause, in response to the call to defend this faith. Obviously, the Faith of Truth must call all humanity to the singular divinity of Allah ﷻ, to the total devotion in all forms of worship to Him alone. Indeed, the raising of this call was the reason behind the sending of all the Messengers, and the revelation of all the Scriptures. But whoever stands against this and rejects it must become the one against which we struggle. Allah ﷻ says:

And fight them until there is no more *Fitnah* (disbelief and polytheism), and the religion will all be for Allah Alone [3]

---

[3] *Al-Anfal*: 39.

And we have already discussed the Prophet's ﷺ Hadith in which he said: "When you meet your enemies, the polytheists, invite them to three things and if they make a positive response to you, accept it and restrain yourselves from doing any harm to them…"

The primary concern of Islam is to call people to what is best; it would be better for them, in the best possible way, to acknowledge truth, but if they refuse we are obliged to fight them. Whenever the freedom of Muslims to call others to embrace Islam is impinged by any despot or *Taaghut*, then he must be brought down so that knowledge of Islam may reach the people, and thus, the principle of: 《**There is no compulsion in religion**》 is applied. That is, should a Muslim ruler come to rule over a particular country, he would not be permitted to press its people to accept Islam as their religion. Their obligation is simply to accept his Islamic political authority. If they choose to become Muslims then their rights are the same as those of any other Muslim and if they choose to keep the religion of their fathers then they must pay *Jizyah* (head tax) or accept that they are in a state of war.[4]

This brings us to the aims of *Jihad*, which are:

1. The Disbelievers should be fought to assure everyone's right to choose between truth and falsehood.

---

[4] See the interpretation of "**There is no compulsion in religion**" in "*Tafsir Ibn Kathir*", Vol.1/459, and The Chapter of *Jihad* in "*Maa'lim fi at-Tariq*", p.74.

2. The Disbelievers should be fought to assure the right of the Muslims to call others to Islam.
3. The Disbelievers should be fought to establish the rule and authority of Islam on earth. This is the supreme liberation of humanity; for it frees them from the worship of human beings; it liberates them from the dark forces of ignorance and from the tyranny of superstition.

Here we have no person, no class, no organisation to legislate and regulate the affairs of nations, to subjugate humanity with the ruse of legality. But human beings have one Lord God whom they all share and who determines for them the Laws by which they must all abide. It is Allah to whom they should all turn in obedience and in awe, in faith and in devotion. [5]

Jihad is also an act of worship, it is one of the supreme forms of devotion to Allah. "If all humanity were believers then *Jihad* would be of no use. Alliance for the Sake of Allah and enmity for His Sake; love for Him and hatred for what He hates would be meaningless. There would be no war upon His enemies, no service to render in guiding people to what is good and dissuading them from iniquity, there would be no virtue in patience nor in steadfastness before the caprice of the spirit, and no goodness in first rendering one's affection to Allah rather than to human beings."[6]

---

[5] *"Tareeq ad-Da'wa"*, Vol.1/288-289.
[6] *"Madaarij as-Salikin"*, Vol.2/196.

Ibn Taymiyyah said: "There is nothing to compare to it (*Jihad*) in terms of merit or reward because everyone benefits from it, both materially and spiritually. It is the expression of all forms of worship, both of the heart and hand. It is inspired by love for Allah, and sincere devotion, by reliance upon Him, and by the spirit of sacrifice both personal and financial. It is patience and hardship, worship in word and in deed, there is nothing which supersedes its blessings. Whoever takes its path, whether a single individual or an entire nation, is assured of success; either to be brought to success and victory, or to receive martyrdom and paradise."[7]

There is much in the sources about this subject. Here are a few of the verses which speak of it in the Qur'an. Allah ﷻ says:

> **Do not think that those who were killed in the way of Allah are dead, indeed they live with their Lord and prosper. They are pleased with what Allah has given them of His Bounty and are glad for those who have not joined them from before, that they shall have no fear and neither shall they grieve** [8]

And,

> **Indeed the true believers are those who believed in Allah and His Messenger, and afterward doubt not but strive with their**

---

[7] "*As-Siyasa ash-Shar'iyya Bayna Ar-Ra'i war-Raiyya*", p.118.
[8] *Aal-Imran*: 169-170.

wealth and their lives for the cause of Allah, these are indeed the truthful [9]

Jihad is also a profitable exchange to be made with Allah, as He ﷻ says:

O You who believe! Shall I tell you of an exchange which will save you from a painful punishment. That you believe in Allah and His Messenger and struggle in the Cause of Allah with your wealth and your lives. This is best for you, if you only knew. He will forgive you your sins and bring you into gardens beneath which rivers flow, a fine abode in Gardens of Eternity, this is the supreme victory. And also another blessing which you love, help from Allah and a near victory, and give glad tidings to the believers [10]

Also in the Sunnah, there are many reports of the merits of *Jihad*, such as the Prophet's ﷺ saying: "Allah has raised up those who struggled in His path by one hundred degrees, and the distance between even two of these is like the distance between the heavens and the earth." [11]   And he said: "Anyone who gets both his feet covered with dust in Allah's Cause will not be touched by the (Hell) fire." [12]   Al-Bukhari reported that a man came to the Messenger of Allah ﷺ and said, "Instruct me as to

---

[9] *Al-Hujuraat*: 15.
[10] *As-Saff*: 10-13.
[11] "*Sahih al-Bukhari*", *The Book of Jihad*, Vol.6/11, Hadith 2790.
[12] "*Sahih al-Bukhari*", *The Book of Jihad*, Vol.6/9, Hadith 2816.

such a deed as equals *Jihad* (in reward)." He replied, "I do not find such a deed." Then he added, "Can you, while a Muslim fighter is in the battlefield, enter your mosque to perform prayers without cease and fast and never break your fast?" The man said, "But who can do that?"[13] Abu Dawud reported that the Prophet 🕮 said: "The tourism of my nation is *Jihad* in the Cause of Allah."[14]

Jihad is the highest expression of Islam, as the Prophet 🕮 has said: "The heart of the matter is Islam, its pillar is *Salah* and its highest achievement is *Jihad*."[15]. And he 🕮 said, "A single endeavor (of fighting) in Allah's cause in the afternoon or in the forenoon is better than all the world and whatever is in it."[16]

At the other end of this we have the humiliation of those who abandon *Jihad*. Those whom Allah has qualified as hypocritical and sick of heart. He 🕮 says:

---

[13] *"Sahih al-Bukhari"*, *The Book of Jihad*, Vol.6/4, Hadith 2785.
[14] *"Sunan Abu Dawud"*, *The Book of Jihad*, Vol.3/12, Hadith 2486, and al-Hakim's *"Mustadrak"*, Vol.2/73. The Hadith is classified as *Hasan*.
[15] *"Sunan Tirmidhi"*, *"Abwab al-Iman"*, Vol.7/281, Hadith 2619, and *"Sunan Ibn Majah"*, Vol.2/1314, Hadith 3973. In his *"Sahih al-Ja'mi' as-Sagheer"*, Vol.5/30, Hadith 5012, Albani classified this Hadith as *Sahih*.
[16] *"Sahih al-Bukhari"*, The Book of *Jihad*, Vol.6/13, Hadith 2792, and *"Sahih Muslim"*, the Book of *al-Imara*, Vol.3/1499, Hadith 1880.

Say, "If your fathers or your sons or your brothers or your wives or kinsmen, or the wealth which you have acquired or the commerce in which you fear a decline, and the dwellings in which you delight - if these are dearer to you than Allah and His Messenger, and striving hard and fighting in His Cause then wait until Allah brings about His Decision (torment). Allah does not guide people who are *Al-Faasiqun* (rebellious, disobedient to Allah)[17]

And Allah also says:

And when a decisive *Surah* is sent down, and *Jihad* is mentioned therein, you will see those in whose hearts is a disease (of hypocrisy) looking at you with a look of one fainting to death. But it was better for them (hypocrites, to listen to Allah and to obey Him). Obedience and good words. And when the matter (preparation for *Jihad*) is resolved on, then if they had been true to Allah, it would have been better for them. Would you then, if you were given authority, do mischief in the land, and sever your ties of kinship? Such are they whom Allah has cursed, so that He has made them deaf and blinded their sight [18]

---

[17] *At-Tawbah*: 24.
[18] *Muhammad*: 20-23.

Jihad is necessary not only for the spread of Islam but it is the way that Allah selects the best and the purest of heart among humanity. Allah ﷻ says:

Do you think that you will enter Paradise before Allah tests those of you who fought in His Cause and tests those who are patient? [19]

And He ﷻ also says:

Do you think that you shall be left alone while Allah has not yet tested those of you who have striven hard and fought and have not taken *Walijah* (helpers, advisors and consultants from disbelievers, pagans, etc. giving openly to them their secrets) besides Allah and His Messenger and the Believers. Allah is well aware of what you do [20]

"*Jihad* in the Cause of Allah is the way in which we call others to Allah, it was not a peculiar response to conditions in the first days of Islam, but rather an inseparable part of the call to truth. If it were only a response to conditions of the times, it would not have been so deeply rooted in the Qur'an and in the Sunnah of the Prophet ﷺ.

---

[19] *Aal-Imran*: 142.
[20] *At-Tawbah*: 16.

Allah knows that *Tawaagheet* despise the very mention of *Jihad*. He ﷺ knows that they will always fight it because it is not their path, nor their law, not only yesterday, but today and tomorrow as well. It will be the same in every time and in every place. Allah knows that evil is braggart and can never be just, it can never let the good thrives even if it resorts to peaceful methods because the prosperity of the good causes a threat to evil. The assertion that truth exists is itself a threat to the existence of falsehood. We recognise the enemy in whatever is wrong. We must know that falsehood can only defend itself by struggling against truth, by throttling it with its bare hands. These are the facts of the matter; it is not a matter of peculiar circumstance, but rather the way of the world. This can only lead to the necessity of *Jihad* in all its forms. Anything conceived of in the mind may finally take form and appear in the real world. The only response to militant evil is an equally militant good. Falsehood fortified must be met with truth ironclad. If this was otherwise then all this would only be foolishness unbefitting the believers. Rather we should devote our lives and our resources the way Allah has required the believers to do."[21]

When the believers realised the meaning of Allah's words,

> **So let those who sell the life of this world for that of the Hereafter fight in the Cause of Allah, and who fights in the Cause of Allah,**

---

[21] *"Tareeq ad-Da'wa"*, Vol.1/303-304.

**and is killed or gets victory, We shall grant
him a mighty reward** [22]

Muslim armies spread across the world spreading
knowledge of Islam and instilling faith in the hearts of
people, they crushed the power of *Taaghut* wherever they
found it so that everyone would be free to worship the
One God. In the early days we find the supreme example
of people who went out in quest of death for the very
love of life. Life which they would enjoy on earth amid
the fruits of victory in the service of the faith, or life with
Allah,

**Do not think that those who were killed in the
Cause of Allah are dead, indeed they live with
their Lord and prosper** [23]

There were some, like the Prophet's Companion
Umair Ibn al-Hammam al-Ansari, for whom the distance
between this world and paradise seemed all too great.
When he heard the Prophet ﷺ at the Battle of Badr call
out "Onward to Paradise, as wide as the heavens and the
earth!" he said, "But Messenger of Allah, is Paradise
really as vast as the heavens and the earth?" "Of course",
the Prophet ﷺ said. "Excellent, excellent!" he said. "Why
do you say that?" the Prophet ﷺ asked. "Nothing but the
hope that I will be one of its people, Messenger of
Allah". Then the Prophet ﷺ told Umair, "You will surely
be one of them". He sat and ate from a bag of dates,
which he had with him, then he said "If I were to live
until I had eaten all these dates of mine, it would be a

---

[22] *An-Nisa'*: 74.
[23] *Aal Imran*: 169.

long life". He tossed them away and threw himself into battle, fighting the enemy until he was killed. [24]

Then there is the story of Handhalah Ibn Abu Aamir who, on hearing the call to war before the Battle of Uhud, rushed out of his house, not even taking the time to have a shower as he was then newly married, but hurried to the fray lest he miss the battle. When he was killed the Prophet ﷺ said: "The Angels are bathing your friend, go and ask his wife". When they asked his wife she said, "He went out as soon as he heard the call to war, not taking the time to cleanse himself of ceremonial impurity". Then the Prophet ﷺ said, "This is why the Angels bathed him."[25]

These are but two of many heroes who were filled to overflowing with faith, who reached the pinnacle of life and were given a glimpse of Paradise and its bounty from where they stood, seeing it as if with their own eyes they flew to it in determined flight as birds return to their roost.[26]

This is the meaning of *Jihad* and these are the believers who make it their road. Whoever follows them does so because they struggle in the Cause of Allah. But,

---

[24] "*Musnad Ahmad*", Vol.3/137, and "Sahih Muslim", "*The Book of al-Imara*", Vol. 3/1509, Hadith 1899, and al-Ghazali's "*Fiqh as-Sirah*", p.244.

[25] Ibn Hajar, "*Al-Isaabah*", Vol.1/360, al-Ghazali's "*Fiqh as-Sirah*", p.272.

[26] See more heroic stories in an-Nadwi's book, "*Ma'da Khasira al-Aalam*", p.104, 108.

as for those who do not, they struggle for the sake of *Taaghut*:

> **Those who believe fight in the Cause of Allah and those who disbelieve fight in the cause of Taaghut** [27]

However, that which the dispirited Muslims today refer to as *Jihad* is nothing other than deception. They call for a truce with the minions of Satan; they call for pacts of unity and alliances with them, and submition to them. They dilute the texts of the Qur'an and the Sunnah to satisfy the doubts of the atheists. They even demand equality for any baseless philosophical speculation which denies divine writ. They are self-defeated, humiliated, subjugated; they do not know nor recognise the truth which is before them; there is nothing of Islam in them but the sound of their names. Their obsession and concern is for blind imitation; their habit is following everybody. However, things would be less worse had they not tried to conceal their cowardice and humiliation and twist the text of the Qur'an and the Sunnah. They say that *Jihad* is only for defense. This lie must be exposed, and we must never relent in denouncing those who make such claims, regardless of who they are, regardless of their popularity or their fame. The religion of Allah is Truth, and Truth never follows tradition nor fashion. There is no need to speak about this here at length. It has been discussed already in earlier chapters and our scholars, both ancient and modern, have spared no effort in exposing this strange belief, throughout the course of

---

[27] *An-Nisa'*: 76.

55

history. Those who are interested will find rich discussion of it in the sources.

Clearly, faith can offer us no rewards until we return to the Qur'an and the Sunnah, and to an understanding of the creed that the Prophet ﷺ himself taught his Companions. We must acquire a knowledge of the lives of the founders of our nation, and take to heart the real meaning of the words: "There is no god but Allah". We must understand the nature of worship; the nature of religion; the nature of *Jihad* for the Sake of Allah, not for the sake of any country, people, race, class, or selfishness.

Muslims today should realise the meaning of this, rise above themselves and feel superior with their Islamic creed. They must take account of the errors of those who are misled and the lies of those who would deceive them. They must turn at every crossing to the Book of Allah and the Sunnah of His Prophet ﷺ and know that they are helpless without the Grace of Allah; that Allah is their Protector and that the ruse of Satan is the very essence of frailty.

The Islamic Ruling regarding Spying on Muslims

A number of scholars have seen it fit to address the question of espionage in the course of their discussions of *Jihad*. Because espionage is the most obvious form of treachery against the Muslims, especially in times of war. Their consideration of it within this context is a revealing point in itself.; therefore I have followed their footsteps and discussed the issue of espionage in the chapter of *Jihad*.

Spying is the ultimate form of treason, and for a Muslim it is a major sin. While it is a form of alliance with the disbelievers, the ruling on it may range from a declaration of disbelief and apostasy to a state of major sinfulness. If its motivation is a longing for the victory of the disbelievers, and a hope for their subjugation of the Muslims, then this is the act of a disbeliever, however if a person was motivated by a desire for some personal or worldly gain or something similar, then it is a major sin.

The story of the Prophet's ﷺ Companion Haatib Ibn Abu Baltaa is often related in this context. He was a veteran of Badr and of Hudaybiyyah, and was sent on the embassy to the Muqawqis, Patriarch of Alexandria and Master of Egypt, who returned him to Madinah together with Maryam, the Copt. He died in the year 30 after the *Hijrah* at the age of 65. Allah ﷻ warned us against espionage in the first verse of Surat *al-Mumtahinah*:

O you who believe! Do not take My enemies and your enemies as friends, showing affection towards them, while they have disbelieved in the truth that has come to you. They have driven the Messenger and yourselves out because you believe in Allah your Lord. If indeed you had gone out to fight in My Cause and to seek My Good Pleasure, then do not confide your affections to them, I am All-Aware of what you conceal and of what you reveal. Whoever among you does this has surely strayed far from the Straight Path [28]

At-Tabari remarked that you must not put yourself in league with your kith and kin, sons or daughters, if they are outside Islam; allying yourself to them and taking them into your hearts, since they could benefit you in no way on the Day of Resurrection, even if they were your closest relations. Those who are mindful of their duty shall enter Paradise and those who deny their obligations and are disobedient shall enter the Fire. [29]

Imam al-Bukhari informs us in the words of Ali Ibn Abu Talib, "Allah's Messenger sent me, Az-Zubair and Al-Miqdad somewhere saying, 'Proceed till you reach the garden of Khakh. There you will find a lady with a letter. Take the letter from her.' So, we set out and our horses ran at full pace till we found the lady and said (to her). 'Hand over the letter.' She replied, 'I have

---

[28] *Al-Mumtahinah*: 1.
[29] *"Tafsir at-Tabari"*, Vol.28/61.

no letter with me.' We said, 'Either you hand over the letter or else we shall remove your clothes.' So, she removed it from her braid. We brought the letter to Allah's Apostle; it contained a statement from Haatib Ibn Abu Baltaa to some of the Makkan pagans, informing them of some of the intentions of Allah's Apostle. Then Allah's Apostle said, 'O Haatib! What is this?' Haatib replied, 'O Allah's Messenger! Don't hasten to give your judgment about me. I was a man closely connected with the Quraish, but I do not belong to this tribe, while the other emigrants with you have their relatives in Makkah who could protect their dependents and property. So, I wanted to recompense for my lacking any blood relation to them by doing them a favour so that they might protect my dependents. I did this neither out of disbelief, nor apostasy, nor out of preferring *Kufr* (disbelief) to Islam.' Allah's Apostle said, 'Haatib has told you the truth.' Umar said, 'O Allah's Messenger! Allow me to chop off the head of this hypocrite.' Allah's Apostle said, 'Haatib participated in the Battle of Badr, and who knows, perhaps Allah has already looked at the Badr warriors and said, 'Do whatever you like, for I have forgiven you." Thus, Allah revealed the above verses.[30]

Ibn al-Qayyim says that the tale of Haatim illustrates the permissibility of killing spies even when they are Muslims, since when Umar wanted to kill Haatib the Prophet 🕮 did not say: "You can't kill a Muslim", rather, he said: "Who knows, perhaps Allah has already looked at the Badr warriors and said, 'Do whatever you

---

[30] *"Sahih al-Bukhari"*, 'The Book of *Tafsir*', *Surat al-Mumtahinah*, Vol.8/633, Hadith 4890.

like'. So his response indicates that Haatib was spared only because he was a veteran of Badr. This leads us to conclude that it is permitted to kill a spy who is not protected by such a circumstance. This is the position of Imam Malik. Imam ash-Sha'fii and Abu Hanifah say that a Muslim spy should not be killed. The Hanbalis are divided, though the opinion of Imam Ahmed appears to be against killing a Muslim spy. Both sides found their arguments in the story of Haatib.

In the final analysis, the decision must be that of the Imam. If the interests of the Muslims are best served by his death then he should be killed, but if these interests are better served by sparing his life then this is what should be done. Allah is best informed of the correct course. [31]

Ibn al-Qayyim added that there is another point raised by the story of Haatib. No matter how great the sin, so long as it is not *Shirk*, the blessings of some other great deed may wipe it away. This is what happened with Haatib whose crime of espionage was forgiven because of his earlier service at Badr, since he had earned the Love of Allah and is Pleasure by his action at Badr. Allah was so pleased with and proud of them that even a crime like espionage would not diminish this and shielded them from the anger of Allah; so the greater merit had overcome the lesser sin. This is a part of Divine Wisdom, He ﷻ determines what is wholesome and what is not, He decrees reward and punishment, He makes the pure heart and the stricken one. And He ﷻ said,

---

[31] Ibnu al-Qayyim, "*Zaad al-Ma'ad*", vol.3/422 with little alteration.

Surely good deeds wipe out evil ones [32]

And Allah ﷻ also said:

If you avoid the evil deeds that have been forbidden to you We will forgive you your transgressions [33]

Ibn al-Qayyim continues by saying, "Perhaps we should consider the depth of faith which lead Haatib to Badr, to put himself in the charge of the Messenger of Allah out of love for Allah and for His Prophet ﷺ, over and above his affection for his family and his tribe, while they had remained in their homes amidst the enemy; his resolve never slackened and his faith never weakened even though it brought him face to face on the field of battle with those who still live with his own kith and kin. But when he was corrupted by the act of spying, the strength of his faith was enough to overcome it, and as his condition worsened he rose to meet it. Thus, when the Prophet ﷺ saw the strength of his faith overcomes his illness (spying), he said: "Who knows, perhaps Allah has already looked at the Badr warriors and said, 'Do whatever you like, for I have forgiven you'".

This is the opposite of the case of Dhul Khuwaysirah at-Tamimi who challenged the Messenger of Allah and those who followed his example; those from among the Khawarij, whose strict observance of their ritual obligations was the envy even of the Companions

---

[32] *Hud*: 114.
[33] *An-Nisa'*: 31.

61

of the Messenger 🕮, but of whom the Messenger said: "If I shall meet them, I will destroy them as the people of 'Aad were destroyed," and also, "Slay them for certainly there is great merit, with Allah, in killing them."[34]

My own thoughts are that Imam Malik, Ibn Aqeel and others from among Imam Ahmad's circle are correct in saying that the Muslim spy should be killed, since the pardon in the case of Haatib was of a kind that could not be applied to anyone else. If it was Islam which had protected him, then it would not have been necessary to grant him any special pardon; because if a ruling is justified by the general, the particular will be of no effect. This seems the more reasonable analysis, although Allah is Most Knowledgeable of the correct course.[35]

This particular revelation begins the words, **⟨O You who believe! Do not take My enemies and your enemies as friends⟩**, referring to Haatib, as a believer. But his example demonstrates the general prohibition, while at the same time the verse seems to suggest that what he did was to ally himself to the disbelievers in some way, and that in doing this he had strayed far from the path. Then the Prophet's response to this: "Haatib has told you the truth, let him go", also clearly indicates that he had not disbelieved, that he was a believer beyond any shadow of doubt, but that he had acted out of some

---

[34] "*Sahih al-Bukhari*", 'The Book of *Manaaqib*', Vol.6/618, Hadith 3611, "*Sahih Muslim*", 'The Book of *Zakat*', Vol.2/746, Hadith 1066.
[35] "*Zaad al-Maa'd*", 3/114.

worldly desire. If he had disbelieved, the Prophet ﷺ would not have said: "Let him go."[36]

As for the disbeliever who is also a spy, such a person must be killed since this is what the Prophet ﷺ did in the case of a spy from among the disbelievers. Ayas Ibn Salamah Ibn al-Akwa' stated that his father told him: "A spy from among the Pagans came to the Prophet ﷺ and sat speaking to his companions for some time, then went on his way. The Prophet ﷺ said, "Go find that man and kill him". So I killed him and stripped him of what he had.[37]

---

[36] Salmaan Ibn Sahmaan, "*Irshaad at-Taalib*", p.15.
[37] "*Sahih al-Bukhari*", 'The Book of *Jihad*', Vol.6/168, Hadith 3051, and Abu Dawud, 'The Book of *Jihad*', Vol.3/112, Hadith 2653.

CHAPTER FOUR: Abandoning Heterodoxy

The abandonment of heterodox sects and innovators is the essence of the doctrine of alliance and dissociation. We have already mentioned in chapter three, of Part One, the position of the Salaf (Rightly guided Caliphs) with regard to innovators, and we have also given a definition of *Bidah* and stressed that some *Bidah* may lead to disbelief while others may not.

Now we will address the issue of avoiding contact with members of these sects. Alliance and dissociation require that we not only denounce their positions but also that we have nothing to do with them on any level. All of our actions must be related to our love for Allah; what He loves we love and what angers Him angers us. The spoiling of one's faith may be attributed to one of two things, or both: either by adopting some unfounded and false belief or practice and engaging in discussion; or behaving in a way which is contrary to the Qur'an and the Sunnah simply in the pursuit of pleasure.

The first of these is *Bidah* or religious innovation. The second is enslavement to desire. These two things constitute the origin of every evil; the beginning of every trial and hardship. It was because of these two things that every Messenger ever sent was rejected; and why people disobeyed their Lord; and thus were condemned to the Fire, or punished at all. Perversion in the realm of belief is the fruit of doubt, but in the realm of action it is the fruit of unrestrained desire. For this reason our forefathers used to say, "Beware of two people; one who is troubled by his own desires, and one who is overwhelmed by his enjoyment of the world."[38]

Also, they used to say, "Beware of the affliction (*fitnah*) of the wicked scholar, and of the ignorant devotee. In them is the source of whatever troubles the righteous. The first are like those who have 'earned the Wrath of Allah', who know the truth but do not act upon it, and the second are like 'those who have gone astray', who act without knowledge of what they do". (the reference is to the last verse of Surat *al-FatihaH*)[39]

The real danger of *Bidah* is that it contradicts "one's submission to Allah Alone". This is why some of the Salaf used to say: "Islam was built upon the solid bedrock of submission."[40] Imam Sufyan at-Thawri used to say that Satan loves *Bidah* more than disobedience, since there is no repentance from *Bidah* while disobedience may be repented for. He said that someone who has introduced something new in religion, sanctioned neither by Allah nor His Messenger, would consider his wrongdoing to be a wonderful thing, so how could he repent from a thing which he thought so well of. Repentance begins with the realisation that something wrong has happened, that there is a need for remorse and

---

[38] Ibnu al-Qayyim, *"I'lam al-Muwaqieen"*, Vol.1/136, Ibn Taymiyyah, *"Iqtidha' as-Sirat al-Mustaqeem"*, p.25.

[39] Ibn Taymiyyah, *"Iqtidha' as-Sirat al-Mustaqeem"*, p.25.

[40] al-Baghawi, *"Sharh as-Sunnah"*, Vol.1/171.

for reform. So long as the nature of an evil deed goes unrecognised, it will not be possible to set it straight.

Having said this, we must also recognise that repentance is always a real possibility for those whom Allah blesses with His Guidance and to whom He reveals the Truth. In this way Allah guides the disbelievers and the hypocrites, the heretics and the shattered sects to the Light of Truth. Allah ﷻ says:

As for those who accept Guidance, He increases their guidance, and bestows on them their piety [41]

As people's ignorance of religion increased the old ways took root once again in their hearts. The bonds of obedience would not hold as people became possessed with pride and love for themselves. It pushed them away from what they knew was right. As one of Salaf said: "No one can abandon any part of the Sunnah without feeling some pride at having done so."[42] We have discussed this earlier mentioning that the enmity between the allies of Allah and the allies of Satan is both natural and inevitable. It arises from the conflict between those who would like to follow the path before them and those who would like to define their own way. Ash-Shawkani says that the reason for this conflict is as clear as daylight. The speculation and invention of the innovator causes those who are faithful to the Messenger to despise them. The hatred of the innovator is a perverse self-

---

[41] *Muhammad*: 17.
[42] Muhammad Ibn Abdul Wahaab, *"Mulhaq Muallafaat"*, p. 87.

hatred projected upon the faithful, because they are faithful and because they are, in the end, right. Indeed the innovators may despise those who follow the Qur'an and the Sunnah faithfully even more than they hate the Christians and the Jews. [43]

Before we discuss in detail the issue of how to avoid the innovators, their novel beliefs and changing fashions, we should perhaps mention something about social intercourse in general. Ibn al-Qayyim, may Allah have Mercy upon him, has spoken of four categories of people with whom interaction is possible:

1- Contact with some people is as necessary as eating; you are perpetually dependent upon them, day and night. When the need arises you seek them out, but when it is satisfied you leave them. These people are as rare as pure gold; as they are the pious, the scholars, and the scourge of Allah's enemies. These bear the Wisdom of Allah and His Messenger, passing on Knowledge of His Book and His Creation. Therefore, any contact with them could only be beneficial.

2- Some people are like medicine, when you are ill you have need of them but when you are well then you do not require them; although you cannot really live without them, you do not need them all the time. Yet if you have enough of them then they may become a burden, like the third group.

---

[43] Ash-Shawkani, "*Qutr al-Wali*", p.259

3- The third class of people are much like varying degrees of inconvenience and affliction. Some are like an incurable disease from which you cannot benefit; for they certainly can do much harm. Some are like a toothache, the pain of which lingers till it has ceased. Some are a source of anxiety and irritation that drives you to your wit's end. They could never help you in any way, and you could never help them. If you speak to them, their words are like clubs beating against the hearts of all who listen. They think that they are as sweet as musk, perfuming the air in pleasant discourse, yet when they cease you feel your spirit soar as if freed from some heavy burden which it could neither bear nor throw down of its own accord. Whoever is afflicted with such people should try to guide them to what is right, until Allah opens a path for your escape.

4- Finally, there is a group who bring nothing but destruction. Contact with them is like taking poison; an antidote is required, but if you do not have it then May Allah help you! These are the heretics and miscreants who obstruct the Way of Allah, and try to twist it to suit themselves. They mould religion to fit their whims, and claim that what they do is the Sunnah of the Prophet ﷺ; but as for the Sunnah that we know, they deny and claim that it is a lie and an invention. For them vice becomes virtue and virtue is in turn considered vice. If you call them to the worship of Allah Alone, they say you have neglected the *Awliya'* and *Salihin* (the saints and righteous ones). If you say, 'Follow none but the Messenger,' they tell you deny and belittle the Imams. If you say that the nature of Allah is as He revealed it to us, and as the Prophet ﷺ has taught us, they fly into a rage shrieking that you have ascribed human qualities to Allah. When you impose the will of Allah and His Messenger and prevent what they have forbidden they say that you are tyrants and demagogues. When you follow the Sunnah and leave what they do aside, they say you are a heretic. If you abandon them completely and consign yourself to Allah they say you feign piety, if you join in with them by following their whims, you would be a fool before Allah and a hypocrite amongst them. Whoever binds himself to the Pleasure of Allah, by opposing those who earn His Ire, has steadfastly bound himself to certainty.[44]

The position of the Muslims with regard to those who follow their own desires and fabrications, while making their claim on Islam, vary according to what they happen to believe. As for those whose *Bidah* has led them into disbelief and *Shirk*, we have nothing at all to do with them and abandon them completely, regarding them as any other disbelievers. This includes people who ordain new rites of worship and consecrate new acts of faith, or who shelter, support and protect an innovator. These people are mentioned in the Hadith, "Whoever introduces an innovation, or gives shelter to a man who introduces an innovation (in religion), is cursed by Allah, by His Angels, and by all the people."[45]

---

[44] *"Bada'i al-Fawa'id"*, Vol.2/274-275.
[45] Abu Dawud, The Book of *ad-Diyat*, Vol.4/669, Hadith 4530, an-Nisa'i, the Book of *al-Qissama*, Vol.8/20. The *Isnad* of this Hadith is *Hasan*.

Ibn al-Qayyim said: "To abandon the Qur'an and the Sunnah and devise a new way to take its place, supporting and praising those who do, and to oppose those who call for observance of the Law of Allah, are some of the greatest crimes of perverse innovation."[46] As for those whose innovations were less than these, who acted within the realms of disobedience and did not reach the frontier of disbelief and *Shirk*, factors of personality and political circumstance would need to be considered also.

We can not encourage others to do what is right, and dissuade them from what is wrong, until we have a clear picture of the entire situation. Failing this, the next best thing is simply to care for oneself, as the Prophet ﷺ has said, "When you see niggardliness being obeyed, desire being followed, worldly interests being preferred, everyone being charmed with his opinion, then care for yourself."[47]

So whenever a Muslim sees someone who is acting disobediently, he should be angry at his evil behaviour but still feel love for what is good in him. We mentioned this earlier during our discussion of the doctrine of *Ahlu Sunnah*. We must not be so vehement in

---

[46] Ibn al-Qayyim, "*I'lam al-Muwaqieen*", Vol.4/405.
[47] Abu Dawud, The Book of *al-Malaahim*, Vol.4/512, Hadith 341, Tirmidhi, The Book of *Tafsir*, Hadith 3060. Tirmidhi classified it as *Hasan Ghareeb*. Ibn Majah, The Book of *Fitan*, Vol.2/1331, Hadith 4014. Albani, though, classifies it as weak. See: "*Mishkaat al-Masaabeeh*", Vol.3/1423.

our condemnation of an evil practice that we ignore the basic goodness of a person and deny him our love. It is possible that being disapproved of and withdrawn from society would cause a person to reform his behaviour and bring himself into line, although it is also possible that it would have no effect, so that he would continue as he was before. The Prophet ﷺ used to avoid those for whom he knew their desertion would have refrained them from innovation, but accepted the excuse of those for whom desertion would have been of no avail, and consigned their secret thoughts to Allah.[48]

In any event, it is not fitting for a Muslim to involve themselves with the heretical, the corrupt or the delinquent, in any way, for if he does he only exposes himself to the retribution of Allah. The least he can do is to forbid their evil deeds, despise their conduct, and hate their innovations according to his power. As the Prophet ﷺ said, "Whoever among you sees an evil deed, let him prevent it with his hand, and if he is unable then let him prevent it with his tongue, and if he is unable then let him prevent it in his heart. This is the smallest degree of faith." [49]

According to the Shari'ah there are two aspects of desertion (*Hajr*):

The first: is the abandonment of evil deeds.

---

[48] "*Ad-Durar as-Sunniyah fi al-Ajwiba an-Najdiyyah*", Vol.7/41.
[49] Ibn Taymiyyah, "*Tafsir Surat an-Nur*", p.55. The Hadith is from "*Sahih Muslim*", 'The Book of *al-Iman*', Vol.1/69, Hadith 49.

The second: is the punishment for these evil deeds.

The first *Hajr* is indicated in the following verses:

And when you see those who engage in a false conversation about Our Verses by mocking at them, stay away from them till they turn to another topics [50]

and Allah's saying:

It has already been revealed to you in the Book (the Qur'an) that when you hear the verses of Allah being denied and mocked at, then sit not with them, until they engage in a talk other than that; certainly in that case you would be like them [51]

This kind of *Hajr* includes also a personal withdrawal from forbidden deeds, as the Prophet ﷺ indicated in the hadith: "The emigrant is someone who avoids what Allah has prohibited." [52] This also forms the motivation of the emigrant, who leaves a place of disbelief and corruption to live in a place of faith and belief, since this is a flight from a situation where one is caught between the disbelievers and the hypocrites and they make it impossible between them for you to fulfill

---

[50] *Al-An'am*: 68.
[51] *An-Nisa'*: 140.
[52] *"Sahih al-Bukhari"*, The Book of *al-Iman*, Vol.1/53, Hadith 10.

your obligations to Allah. This is why Allah ﷻ says: ﴾And evil shun﴿, (74:5).

The second *Hajr* is a punitive response given to those who involve themselves in evil deeds, until they repent. In this way the Prophet ﷺ and the Muslims deserted, "the three people who stayed behind", and continued to do so until Allah confirmed their repentance. (A detailed discussion of this incident will follow in part 4).

Precisely what action is to be taken will differ according to the strength and number of those involved. The idea is to apply pressure for reform, whether great or small. If severe pressure or ostracism will result in a weakening or suppression of destructive and antisocial behaviour then this should be the appropriate response, but if this results in a deepening of the problem, then it is not the correct response. So in some situations a gentler form of correction is required. But regardless of the choice here, it is first necessary to recognise that what is done is purely for the sake of Allah. Whoever acts of his own accord, in response to his own desire, or who acts in any way other than that which is prescribed, has stepped outside the bounds of this principle. There is no greater deception than that of someone who confuses his own dictates with Divine Will."[53]

We are in fact dealing here with "punishments based on the Shari'ah Law". This is a type of *Jihad* in the way of Allah. The reason for doing this is in order to

---

[53] Ibn Taymiyyah, *"Majmu' al-Fatawa"*, Vol.28/203-207.

assure the supremacy of the Word of Allah, to ensure that religion is entirely for the Sake of Allah. Whoever believes in it must make his enemies or friends for the Sake of Allah. Whoever is a believer must be the ally of a believer, even if he is guilty of some transgression against his brother. The injustice of one action does not negate the responsibility of standing beside him in faith. Allah ﷻ has said:

> **And if two groups among believers fight, then seek a settlement between them, but if a group of them rebels against the other, then fight you against the one which rebels till it complies with the command of Allah; then if it complies, make reconciliation between them justly and be equitable. Verily! Allah loves those who are equitable. The believers indeed are brothers. So make reconciliation between your brothers**
> [54]

Here Allah ﷻ considers them brothers even when they fight against each other.[55]

There is a final comment which should be noted: "The groups which we avoid and dissociate ourselves from completely, whom we oppose openly, are those who differ with us over very fundamental aspects of faith; it does not include simple differences of opinion amongst the scholars, over the finer points of the law. We see these minor differences as a blessing which Allah has

---

[54] *Al-Hujuraat*: 9-10.
[55] Ibn Taymiyyah, *"Majmu' al-Fatawa"*, Vol.28/208.

bestowed upon humanity, in order that religion would not become a burden upon us. Such differences existed even among the Companions of the Prophet ﷺ, who were closer than brothers and respected one another deeply. After them, groups of scholars referred to one or another of their opinions, as a source and authority, for their own decisions. All of them were seeking truth, all of them followed the Path of Guidance, all of them were thankful to Allah for the understanding they were given". [56]

---

[56] Al-Baghawi, "*Sharh as-Sunnah*", Vol.1/229.

A Word from the Salaf about Adherence to the Qur'an and Sunnah and Abstention from Innovation

The first generations of the Muslims observed the Qur'an and the Sunnah strictly. They were severe in their treatment of anyone who diverged from these two fundamental sources of guidance. They spoke often of this; so it is perhaps fitting here to relate some of what they used to say, both to remind ourselves of their example and to encourage each other to follow it.

Imam Malik said: "Whoever introduces something new to this religion, which those who came before him did not observe, must contend that the Messenger of Allah ﷺ has betrayed the faith, since Allah has said: ❴**Today I have completed for you your religion**❵ (5:3). Whatever was not part of religion on that day, is no part of it today."[57]

Ibn Mas'oud ﷺ said, "You will find people calling you to the Book of Allah, though they themselves have rejected it completely. You must seek knowledge, beware of the innovator, the intransigent and the entrenched. Always go back to the very beginning."[58]

Abu al-Aaliyyah ar-Riyahi said: "Learn Islam, and once you know it then do not stray from it. You must keep to the Straight Path. Islam is the unswerving way, do not

---

[57] Ash-Shaatibi, "*Al-I'tisaam*", Vol.2/53.
[58] Al-Malti, "*At-Tanbeeh War-Radd*", p.85.

bend it to the right nor to the left. You must keep to the Sunnah of your Prophet and his Companions." [59]

Imam ash-Sha'fii said: "It is better for someone to come to Allah with every sort of sin there is, other than *Shirk*, than to come to him with any sort of obedience to whims."[60]

Sufyan Ibn Uyaynah was asked: "Why do the followers of whims have a great love for their whims?" He replied: "Have you forgotten what Allah ﷻ said: **⟨And their hearts absorbed the calf because of their disbelief⟩**, (2:93). [61]

Abu Qallaba said, "Do not associate with the people of heretic tendencies, for you can not avoid being immersed in their wrongdoing nor prevent them confusing you in what you have little knowledge of."[62]

Ibn Mas'oud ﷺ said, "Follow and do not innovate, this will be enough." [63]

And so today, the Book of Allah is clear and the Sunnah of His Prophet ﷺ is plain and stands as a guide and exposition of the Qur'an itself. The history of Islam and the first generations of the Muslims have been preserved for us. There is nothing more for us to do other

---

[59] Ibid. p. 84.

[60] Al- Bayhaqi, *"Al-I'tiqaad Ala Mad'hab as-Salaf"*. p.118.

[61] Ibn Taymiyyah, *"Al-Ubudiyya"*, p. 70.

[62] Al- Bayhaqi, *"Al-I'tiqaad Ala Mad'hab as-Salaf"*. p.118.

[63] *"Sunnan ad-Darami"*, 'The Book of *al-Ilm'*,Vol.1/69.

than to follow the Book and the Sunnah, to steer clear of all innovation and novelty. If we would only do this then our Ummah would be singularly distinguished among humanity and also independent unto itself. Those whose minds are full of wishes and those whose hearts are full of design would be unable to impose upon us any human deficiency. There was never a nation which followed its nose without falling into a turbulent foolishness and final destruction. Allah wants His servants to stand in the Light with security and happiness. This comes only from Islam, whatever opposes these things is only ignorance and falsehood. From it we seek the protection of Allah.

CHAPTER FIVE: Severance of Marriage and Inheritance between Muslims and Disbelievers

Muslims may not inherit from non-Muslims; in this way one of the bonds of kinship between Muslims and their non-Muslim relatives has been severed. For an understanding of why this is, we must examine the principles of alliance and dissociation from an Islamic perspective.

The prohibition with regard to marriage with disbelievers was imposed only after the revelation of the order to make *Jihad*. Ibn al-Qayyim mentioned that before *Jihad* was imposed, the Prophet ﷺ acknowledged that Muslims could remain with their spouses whom they had married before Islam, though they tried to get them to convert. Even though a woman may have been a Muslim and her husband a disbeliever, the Shari'ah did not separate them, not at least until the Treaty of Hudaibiyyah, after which marriage between Muslim women and disbelievers was prohibited [64]. Allah ﷻ says:

They are not lawful (wives) for the disbelievers nor are the disbelievers lawful (husbands) for them[65]

and He ﷻ also says:

---

[64] *"Ahkaam Ahl adh-Dhimmah"*, Vol.1/69.
[65] *Al-Mumtahinah*: 10.

Likewise hold not the disbelieving women as wives[66]

So it was firmly established that there would be no ties between Muslims, other than those of faith; there would be no obligations other than those imposed by religion, and that all bonds would be with those who bound themselves to Allah.[67]

The prohibition of marrying a disbeliever was mentioned again in Surat al-Baqarah,

And do not marry (*Al-Mushrikaat*) pagan women until they believe. And indeed a slave woman who believes is better than a (free) pagan woman, though she may please you. And give not (your daughters) in marriage to pagan men until they believe and verily, a believing slave is better than an (free) idolater, though he may please you. Those (pagans) invite you to the Fire, and Allah invites you to Paradise and Forgiveness by His Leave, and makes His Signs clear to mankind that they may remember[68]

Shaikh Abdur Rahman Ibn Sa'di, may Allah have mercy upon him, said with regard to the Verse: ❨**Do not marry pagan women**❩: this establishes a general principle which applies to all unbelieving women. This

---

[66] *Al-Mumtahinah*: 10.
[67] Sayyid Qutb, "*Adh-Dhilal*", 6/3546.
[68] *Al-Baqarah*: 221.

was later clarified further with the revelation of the dispensation for marriage with women from among the People of the Book, **《and the chaste women from those who were given the Scripture (lawful to you in marriage》**[69]. As for Allah's Verse: **《Do not marry pagan men until they believe》**, no exceptions were ever indicated and so the general prohibition remains.

In the course of prohibiting Muslims to marry those who are outside their religion Allah reminds us that, **《Those (pagans) invite you to the Fire》**. In their words and deeds, in the style of their lives they represent a constant threat and an unyielding peril to a believer in their midst.[70]

As Ibn Taymiyyah points out, all the scholars are agreed that it is permitted for Muslim men to marry women from among the People of the Scripture, but it is also reported that Ibn Umar discouraged marriage with Christian women, saying he did not know of a greater kind of Shirk than that of someone who says that our Lord is Jesus, the son of Mary.[71] However, there are three arguments against Ibn Umar's disapproval of such marriages:

The first is that the People of the Scripture are not Pagans since Allah says: **《Indeed those who believe and**

---

[69] *Al-Ma'idah*: 5.

[70] Ibn Sa'di, *"Tafseer Kalam al-Mannaan"*, Vol.1/274.

[71] "Sahih Al-Bukhari", (Vol.9/416, Hadith 5385), 'The Book of Divorce', Chapter: Allah's verse: **"Do not marry pagan women until they beleieve"**.

those who are Jews and the Christians and the
Sabaens⟩, *Al-Baqarah*: 62. Some may maintain that they
have been called *"Mushrik"* (idolaters) in the Qur'an,

> **They (Jews and Christians) took their rabbis
> and their priests as lords besides Allah, and the
> Messiah, son of Mary, while they were
> commanded only to worship none but One
> God, none has the right to be worshipped but
> He. Praise and Glory be to Him, from having
> the partners they associate with
> Him** [72]

But they are not really Pagans since Allah sent all
of His messengers with the message of the divine unity
of God. But the Christians later introduced pagan
doctrines into their faith; yet while they may appear to be
pagan in their beliefs, the foundation of their religion still
rests upon obedience to a revealed scripture.

The second point is that the verse in Surat *al-Baqarah*
establishes a general rule but that in Surat *al-Ma'idah* is
specific; the specific always takes precedence over the
general.

Thirdly, one could maintain that the verse in Surat *al-Ma'idah* actually abrogates the prohibition in Surat *al-Baqarah* since all scholars agree that *al-Ma'idah* was
revealed after *al-Baqarah*. [73]

---

[72] *At-Taubah*: 31.
[73] Ibn Taymiyyah, *"Daqaaiq at-Tafseer"*, Vol.1/258-260.

82

It appears to me that the first of these points which Ibn Taymiyyah mentioned is not firmly established, albeit that the origin of the Christian religion is indeed *Tawhid*. They have in fact contradicted this principle in the course of the evolution of their religion. The other two points are supported by most of the scholars.[74]

As for inheritance, it too is an aspect of alliance and dissociation. The authority for it comes from the hadith of the Prophet ﷺ: "The disbeliever does not inherit from the Muslim, and neither does the Muslim from the disbeliever".[75]

The reason for this is that inheritance is related to alliance and dependence and the Qur'an states that there can be no such relation between Muslims and disbeliever. Allah ﷻ says:《**Do not take the Jews and the Christians as protectors they protect one another**》.[76] Al-Baghawi said: "The majority of the scholars from among the Sahabah held to this premise, that the disbeliever did not inherit from the Muslim and that the Muslim could not inherit from the disbeliever, because of the severance of relations between them. Some of the Companions, however, such as Mua'wiyya and Maadh held that the disbeliever could not inherit from the Muslim, but the Muslim could inherit from the disbeliever. Ibrahim an-Nakhahi held the same opinion. Similarly, a Muslim man

---

[74] Ibnu Qudaamaa, "*Al-Mughni*", Vol.7/129.
[75] Al-Bukhari, *K. al-Fara'id*, Vol.12/50, (6764), Muslim, *K. al-Fara'id*, Vol.3/1233 (1614).
[76] "*Fath al-Bari*", Vol.12/50.

could marry women from the People of the Book, but no man from amongst them could marry a Muslim woman. This opinion was held by Ishaaq Ibn Rahuyah."[77]

The apostate can not inherit from anyone; Muslim, disbeliever or apostate. With regard to his own estate, there are a variety of opinions. One group maintains that no one can inherit from him; his estate is booty. This is the position of Imam Malik and ash-Sha'fi'i. Another hold that his estate goes to his Muslim heirs, this is the opinion of al-Hasan, ash-Sha'bi, Omar Ibn Abdul Aziz, Awza'i', Abu Yusif and Muhammad. Others say that the wealth which he earned while he was a Muslim will go to his Muslim heirs, but not that which he earned after his apostasy. This is the opinion of Sufyan ath-Thawri and Abu Hanifa.[78]

Every Muslim should find distinction and honour in his religion; it should elevate him above whatever and whoever takes issue with the fundamental principles upon which it is founded. In fact he should have no connection with anything which may hold him back, shake his faith or expose him to hypocrisy. For this reason marriage to disbelieving men was forbidden since no Muslim should ever be placed under the authority or protection of a disbeliever. Muslims should dominate and not be dominated by others. Likewise, Muslim men are warned not to marry disbelieving women because of the danger which they pose, threatening to draw them into their community and to rear their children in a culture of

---

[77] *"Sharh as-Sunnah"*, Vol.8/364.
[78] Ibid., Vol.8/365.

disbelief. Inheritance from disbelievers was prohibited in order to protect Muslims from the taint of the ill-gotten gains of his disbelieving kin who would be pleased with his own wrongdoing and proud of his defiance to the Shari'ah.

So while alliance and mutual support are outside the realms of possible relations between Muslims and disbelievers generally, the prohibition of bonds of marriage and inheritance with them is of the first order, since it is primarily concerned with the consecration of one's life to Allah alone, to observance of His Wisdom and Guidance and compliance with His Law.

In this way Muslims distinguish themselves from all others. They worship none other than Allah, their lives are in His Hands alone, they put their hopes in none but Him, and ask none but Him to satisfy their needs. They will not attribute even the smallest thing to anything other than the Will of Allah, as this is essentially the meaning of submission to Allah; obedience to Him and following His Way.

CHAPTER SIX: Prohibition of Imitating the Disbelievers and the Assertion of Islamic Identity

Our religion does not set Muslims apart from others simply for appearance's sake. Rather, it does this in order to create an independent Islamic identity in the minds of the believers, and to strengthen the idea of an Islamic Society in the eyes of the public generally. It is part of our belief that we should not resemble the disbelievers, neither in appearance nor in action. This is a frequently mentioned subject both in the Qur'an and the Sunnah. The reason for this restriction is that open resemblance to the disbelievers must naturally lead to a resemblance in belief, to empathy with the disbelievers and to affection for them. Finally, we find an approval of the disbelievers' approach to faith as an extension of their own desires. When this happens Muslims are put at risk; when they can no longer distinguish between themselves and others, then they will follow every passing fashion.

This is contrary to Allah's wish, which is to raise the Muslims up and honour them. If we look at the issue in terms of the revelation of the Qur'an, we will find that the first Muslims received a long apprenticeship in the fundamental doctrines of faith before any obligations were placed upon them. Once this had taken root in the hearts of the people, then their obligations were revealed one after the other. Gradually their faith was built up to its final summit.

This is why the Muslims were not ordered to distinguish themselves from the disbelievers until after the *Hijrah*. This measure was taken when *Jihad* was prescribed so as to insure the safety and security of the new Islamic Society from every possible threat, and to bring into being a unique Islamic personality. This creed is unique in its style and in its message; in the image it projects and in the very appearance of those who embrace it. Whoever professes it is raised by it in distinction, as Allah has taken him out of darkness and into light.

The Muslim World today is subject to violent assaults from all sides, resulting from their emulation of the disbelieving Western World, with their weakness of faith, who claim to be the only road to development and progress. On this subject Muhammad Asad says, "Only very superficial people can believe that it is possible to imitate a civilisation in its external appearance without being at the same time affected by its spirit. A civilisation is not an empty form but a living organism. As soon as we begin to adopt the outward forms of that organism, its inherent currents and dynamic influences set to work in ourselves and mould slowly, imperceptibly, our whole moral attitude. It is in perfect appreciation of this truth that the Prophet ﷺ said, 'Whoever imitates other people becomes one of them'[79]. This well-known Hadith is not only a moral admonition but also an objective statement of fact - in this case, the fact of the inevitability of the

---

[79] *"Sunan Abu Dawud"*, Vol.4/413, Hadith 4031, *The Book of Dress*, and *"Musnad Ahmad"*, Vol.7/142, Hadith 5114. Ahmad Shakir said the *Sanad* of this Hadith is *Sahih*; Albani classifies it as *Sahih*.

Muslims being assimilated by any non-Muslim civilization which they imitate in its external form.

In this respect, it is hardly possible to find a fundamental difference between "important" and "unimportant" aspects of social life. Nothing is unimportant in this context. There can be no greater mistake than to suppose that dress, for example, is something purely "external" and, thus, of no importance to the intellectual and spiritual nature of man. Dress is generally the outcome of an age-long development of a people's tastes and needs. Its fashion corresponds to the aesthetic conceptions of that people, and its inclinations. It has been shaped and is constantly being re-shaped according to the changes through which the character and the inclinations of its people are passing. Western fashions of today, for instance, correspond to the intellectual and moral character of the modern West.

By adopting Western dress in place of his own, the Muslim unconsciously adapts his tastes to those of the West and twists his own intellectual and moral Self in such a way that it ultimately "fits" the new dress. And in doing so he renounces a good deal of the cultural possibilities open to his own people; he renounces their traditional tastes, their aesthetic valuations, their likes and dislikes, and accepts the livery of intellectual and moral serfdom to a foreign civilization.

In other words, if a Muslim imitates the dress, the manners and the mode of life of the West, he betrays his preference for his civilization, whatever his avowed pretensions may be. It is practically impossible to imitate a foreign civilization without appreciation of its spirit. It is equally impossible to appreciate the spirit of a civilization which is opposed to a religious outlook on life, and yet remain a good Muslim. The tendency to imitate a foreign civilization is invariably the outcome of a feeling of inferiority."[80]

Allah has created in humanity, and in all things, a natural dynamic attraction. The closer things resemble one another the more intense the attraction becomes. The common bond between human beings makes the attraction between them stronger; because of this, people exert a strong influence upon one another in terms of social behaviour. As for superficial resemblance, these naturally involve a more subtle and more gradual process of assimilation at a deeper level. We have seen that Christians and Jews who live among Muslims are less profound in their disbelief than those who do not. By the same token, we see that Muslims who live among Jews or Christians are weaker in faith than those who do not.[81]

Finally, the common bond of resemblance brings about a feeling of harmony and concord, across time and space. It gives rise to a species of love and affection in the heart; in the same way love of the heart can inspire physical resemblance.

If resemblance in worldly matters will engender mutual love and devotion, what should we expect of

---

[80] Muhammad Asad, "Islam at the Crossroads".
[81] "Iqtidaa' as-Siraat al-Mustaqeem", p.22.

resemblance in religious matters? Certainly they lead to even deeper and stronger devotion, and to a love that locks out faith, as Allah has said,

> **O You who believe, do not take the Jews and the Christians as protectors, they only protect one another. Whoever takes them as protectors is surely one of them. Indeed Allah does not guide an unjust people** [82]

The sealing of an alliance with them can only be accomplished by a negation of faith; when faith is no longer necessary it can not be said to exist. Therefore, we would like to present some of the many references of this from the Qur'an and the Sunnah that make it clear that resembling the disbelievers and following their whims is not permitted in Islam. Allah ﷻ says,

> **Then We have set you (Muhammad) on a clear road of (Our) commandment; so follow it, and follow not the whims of those who know not. Verily, they can avail you in no way against Allah. Verily, the wrong-doers are protectors to one another; but Allah is the Protector of the pious** [83]

Ibn Taymiyyah says in his 'Tafseer' of this verse that Allah had commanded Prophet Muhammad ﷺ only to follow His Commandment, but not the opinions of those who do not know. Anyone who differs with the

---

[82] *Al-Ma'idah*: 51.
[83] *Al-Jaathiya*: 18-19.

Shari'ah is included in "**those who do not know**". Their 'opinion' includes everything the disbelievers hold to be important; the attitudes inspired by their religion and the obligations it places upon them. To reach an agreement with them over these things is to follow their view of things. This is why the disbelieves are always pleased when the Muslims agree with them about something, taking great delight in it.

If it is so that we are required not to follow their wishes, then there could be no doubt that differing with them is the more decisive course to follow in this regard, and thus more sure pleasing Allah.[84] Evidence for this is found in Surat *al-Baqarah*, Allah 🙶 says:

Never will the Jews nor the Christians be pleased with you until you follow their religion. Say, "Indeed the Guidance of Allah is the only Guidance", but if you followed their desires after what had come to you of knowledge from Allah, then you would have in Him no Ally and no helper [85]

Observe how the verse is phrased; it uses "*Millatahum*" (their religion), and then in the prohibition it uses "*Ahwa'ahum*" (their desires). The Jews and the Christians will never be pleased with you until you follow them in everything. The rebuke in this verse is for following what the disbelievers want, whether in small things or in big things. Everyone recognises that

---

[84] "*Iqtidaa' as-Siraat al-Mustaqeem*", p.14.
[85] *Al-Baqarah*: 120.

following part of what they believe is the same as following part of what they prefer, or part of what they are likely to prefer.[86]

The evidence from the Qur'an appears in Surat *al-Baqarah* with reference to the change of the Qiblah from Jerusalem to the Ka'bah at Makkah. Allah ﷻ says,

> **And even if you were to bring to the people of the Scripture all kinds of proof, they would not follow your Qiblah, nor are you going to follow their Qiblah. And they will not follow each other's Qiblah. Verily, if you follow their desires after that which you have received of knowledge, then indeed you are one of the wrong-doers...(until)... And from wherever you start forth (for prayers), turn your face in the direction of *Al-Masjid-al-Haraam* (at Makkah); and wherever you are, turn your faces towards it (when you pray) so that men may have no argument against you, except those of them that are wrong-doers, so fear them not, but fear Me! - And so that I may complete My Blessing upon you and that you may be guided [87]**

More than one of our predecessors said that this means that the Jews could not dispute with the Muslims over the Qiblah. The Jews would then say: "The Muslims had agreed with us over the Qiblah, and so they almost

---

[86] "*Iqtidaa' as-Siraat al-Mustaqeem*", p.15.
[87] *Al-Baqarah*: 145-150.

agreed with us over our religion. Then Allah declared their divergence over the Qiblah and explained that one of the reasons for the abolition of the first Qiblah and the appointment of another was to differ with the disbelievers over it, exposing those who yearn for falsehood. This is the real point behind every agreement and disagreement: If the disbelievers seem to agree with the Muslims over anything, it is sure to be something they believe in anyway, or that which is close to a belief of theirs, as was the case with the Jews when they agreed with the Muslims over the first Qiblah.[88]

Allah has forbidden resemblance with the disbelievers in any way or fashion. He ﷻ says:
Keep both of you to the Straight Way and do not follow the path of those who know not [89]
And,
Do not follow the way of the mischief-makers[90]
And He says:
And whoever opposes the Messenger after having been shown guidance and follows a path other than that of the believers We shall keep him in the path he has chosen, and burn him in Hell - what an evil destination [91]

All that stands as proof that to differ with the disbelievers, abandoning any resemblance to them, is to obey the Commandment of Allah.

---

[88] *"Iqtidaa' as-Siraat al-Mustaqeem"*, p.16.
[89] *Yunus*: 89.
[90] *Al-A' raaf*: 142.
[91] *An-Nisa'* : 115.

93

As for the Sunnah, there has been much related about this subject, including the Prophet's Hadith, "Whoever resembles a people is one of them". Ibn Taymiyyah comments on this Hadith saying that its *Isnad* is Good and that it relates to the prohibition of resembling the disbelievers in their appearance as this represents disbelief and is evidence of the same; as Allah has said in Surat *al-Ma'idah*, verse 51:

❨Whoever takes them as protectors is surely one of them❩.

This is the gist of what Abdullah Ibn Amru said: "Whoever settles in the land of the disbelievers, celebrates their holidays and festivals, resembles them and dies among them will be gathered together with them on the Day of Resurrection."[92] It could be that this relates to a total resemblance which involves disbelief; or it could be that it relates to a degree of resemblance to them, whether out of disbelief or disobedience, in sympathy with disbelief or with disobedience: then one would be judged accordingly.

However, people can be seen doing the same things though they are not in fact imitating one another. There are several views of this kind of resemblance. The Prophet ﷺ, however, did forbid this, so that there would be no possible excuse for imitating disbelief, and no scope for disagreement over it. Evidence for this is found in the Hadith: "You will follow the ways of those nations

---

[92] *"Iqtidaa' as-Siraat al-Mustaqeem"*, p.83.

who were before you, span by span and cubit by cubit (i.e., inch by inch), so much so that even if they entered a hole of a mastigure, you would follow them." We said, "O Allah's Apostle! (Do you mean) the Jews and the Christians?" He said, "Whom else?"

Ibn Omar narrated that: "Some people had gone with the Prophet ﷺ to a place called *al-Hijr* - in the land of Thamud - they took water from one of its wells and prepared some porridge, but the Prophet ﷺ told them to pour out the water and to give the porridge to the camels and instructed them to use the well reserved for livestock."[93]

Imam Ahmad reports that the disbelievers had a tree upon which they used to hang their arms, calling it the "Tree of Honour". Some people came to the Prophet ﷺ saying, "Messenger of Allah. Make us a 'Tree of Honour' like they have. He replied, "Allahu Akbar! You have said the same thing Musa's people said when they asked him to make them a god like (the disbelievers') god, surely these traditions are built upon those ways of the people who came before you; you will indeed follow the ways of those nations who were before you."[94] It was but the imitation of the disbelievers, in taking a particular tree to sit under and hang their weapons on, that the Prophet ﷺ condemned. So what about less trivial resemblance in clear acts of 'Shirk'? [95]

---

[93] "Sahih Muslim", Vol.4/2285, Hadith 2981.
[94] "*Musnad Ahmad*", Vol.5/218. Its *Isnad* is Sahih, and the transmitters are authentic (Sahih).
[95] "*Iqtidaa' as-Siraat al-Mustaqeem*", p.314.

Which is more significant; hanging your arms on a particular tree, prohibited in its imitation of the disbelievers, or the adoption of an entire way of life, with all its laws defining what is permitted and what is not? So what is required and what is prescribed for those who transgress their bounds?

There are other Ahadith in which the Prophet ﷺ prohibits imitation: "The Jews and the Christians do not dye (their grey hair); so you shall do the opposite of what they do (i.e. dye your grey hair and beards)."[96] And he ﷺ said, "Act differently from the Jews; for they do not pray in their sandals or their shoes."[97] He ﷺ also said: "Whoever imitates any other than us is not one of us."[98]

This should suffice to dispel any arguments or excuses expressing that open imitation may be excused on the grounds of common goals or deeds. But still, there may be times when Muslims could imitate disbelievers in their external appearances. So when is it that we may agree or differ? Abul Abbas Ahmad Ibn Taymiyyah answers this question saying, "The Muslims did not diverge from the disbelievers (in such matters) until after the victory of the faith and its emergence as a power: The beginning of *Jihad*, the imposition of *Jizyah* and tribute.

---

[96] "Sahih al-Bukhari", Vol.6/496, Hadith 3462, and "Sahih Muslim", Vol.3/1663, Hadith 2103.
[97] "Sunan Abu Dawud", Vol.1/427, Hadith 652, *The Book of Salat*. Albani classifies it as *Sahih*, "*Sahih al-Ja'mi*'", Vol.3/106, Hadith 3205.
[98] "Sunan at-Tirmidhi", Vol.7/335, Hadith 2696; at-Tirmidhi said its *Isnad* is *Daeef* (weak), but Albani classifies it as *Hasan*, see "*Sahih al-Ja'mi*'", Vol.5/101, Hadith 531.

However, when the Muslims were weak, in the early days, they were not required to differ from the disbelievers; but with the completion of the Faith, when it was raised up and asserted itself, then this was done."

These words were addressed seven hundred years ago, but what about our situation today? Muslims who are in the "Land of War" or the "Land of Disbelief" when there is no war, the obligation to differ from the disbelievers does not always apply, for it could be that necessity dictates otherwise. Indeed, it could be preferable, or even at times required to appear to be similar to them, if this is in the best interests of their mission which is to call others to Islam, or to conceal their identity from their enemies, or to deflect some harm or hardship which threatens the Muslim community and so on. But as for the "Land of Islam and the *Hijrah*" which Allah has blessed with His Faith, where He has imposed both *Jizyah* and tribute upon the disbelievers, here differing with them is required.

If over the passage of time the Muslims came to resemble or differ from the disbelievers, then the Prophet's words have come to pass. The scholars have mentioned a golden rule, around which revolves Allah's Shari'ah and to which all matters originate, in the words of Ibn al-Qayyim, "The weightier principle must always prevail, even if this means that the lesser of them is to be sacrificed; the lesser evil is to be preferred to the greater of the two. The lesser principle vanishes before the greater, and the lesser evil repels the greater one."[99]

However, a word of warning is appropriate here, as a Muslim could not find his way in this matter, other than by the Guidance of Allah who moves the heart of His Servant to its course. His sole motivation must be to follow the example of the Prophet ﷺ; his sole desire must be to do what is right by Allah, and most pleasing to Him and most likely to earn His favour.[100]

As for differing with the People of the Book, the three major points of guidance are as follows:[101]

(1) As for those points which are shared between the two revealed laws, or which were revealed to us while they practiced the same thing, such at the Fast of *Ashuraa'*, or for prayers and fasting generally; the difference lies in the degree of our observance. The Sunnah for the Fast of *Ashuraa'*, for example, is to fast on the ninth and tenth of the month of Muharram. Likewise we were told to make haste to brake our fast, in order to differ from the people of the Book. By the same token we delay the last meal, before the beginning of the fast, to differ from them. We may pray in our shoes, unlike the Jews who may not, and so on. There are many examples of this in the realm of custom and ritual.

---

[99] *"Al-Jawāab al-Kafee"*, p.167.

[100] *"Bada'i' al-Fawa'id "*, Vol.2/262.

[101] Ibnu Taymiyyah mentioned the three points in *"Iqtidaa' as-Siraat al-Mustaqeem"*, p.178-179.

(2) There are observances which were ordained but later abrogated, like the Sabbath, or occasions for special prayers or fasting. Following them in these things is clearly prohibited. Their festivals, for example, are observed by obligatory or voluntary rituals which are not observed at other times. This may be prayer, remembrance, giving of alms, or the performance of certain rites. Other things may be done specially to mark the occasion, out of deference to custom or to win the esteem of others, such as distributing food or clothing to the poor. For our part we have just two Eids, or festivals. In both of them there is a special prayer; one Eid is marked by special almsgiving and the other with the sacrifice of an animal, in both cases for the provision of food. To agree with them over something which was abolished is worse than to agree with them over whichever of our observances share a common origin. For this reason, celebrating these holidays is forbidden to us; while celebrating, with them, those that are shared between us is "*Makruh*" (abominable).

(3) Sharing with them in the festivals which they have themselves invented is worst of all. If the Muslims should invent a festival this is bad enough, yet how could the disbelievers invent such a thing for us? Rather it is a *Bida'* of the disbelievers, which is how it should be seen. There is one final point, whatever Muslims do in their customs and their rituals of worship that resembles the worship and customs of the disbelievers is something which the Muslims themselves have introduced into religion, it is *Bida'*, so long as it can not be attributed to anyone other than them. But whatever is part of our

Shari'ah, whatever the first generations of the Muslims used to do, is beyond reproach.

In short, to celebrate with them in the first instance is abominable, in the second it is *Haram* and in the third it is doubly *Haram*.

Aspects of the Relation between Imitation and Alliance

There is nothing beneficial, which Allah has not pointed out to us, and there is nothing harmful which He has not warned us against. He has commanded us to differ from the disbelievers in their fashion, and there is great wisdom in this: [102]

(1) By sharing in an outward fashion, a harmony of form arises between two things which resemble one another. This harmony leads to a similar level of worldly conduct, regarding outward appearance. Thus, the uniform of a combat soldier, for instance, induces the person who wears it to behave in a certain way; his personality will also be affected by this, unless something else prevents this.

(2) On the other hand, differing with these fashions and styles stresses the fundamental differences between things and protects the Muslim from falling into the displeasure of Allah and from wandering astray. It brings his heart near to those who are guided and who seek the pleasure of Allah. It affirms the division which Allah has decreed between those who are allied in His service and those who are ranged against Him. Therefore, the depth of one's sincerity of belief and knowledge of what Islam really is - not just adopting the appearance of a Muslim, nor just following a traditional belief in one's heart - will be reflected in one's feeling of differing with

---

[102] *"Iqtidaa' as-Siraat al-Mustaqeem"*, p. 11-12.

the Jews and the Christians, both in one's heart and outward appearance, and avoiding any adoption of their behaviour.

(3) Finally, participating in their fashions and styles requires you to mix freely with them, in the end it becomes impossible to tell between who is Muslim and who is not. If this was really only a matter of personal preference, then you would find many outward similarities with them. But disbelief is a basic part of their behaviour, approving of it and adopting it yourself is in fact the adoption and approval of a type of falsehood and rebellion against Allah, which one should be aware of.[103]

Study in Similarities

Every nation has its distinguished Festivals, so this is a good place to start when speaking about similarities between the Muslims on the one hand, and the Jews and the Christians on the other. Much has been related about the prohibition of following them in this matter, from the **Book**, the **Sunnah**, the *Ijma'* (consensus) and from the **Qiyaas** (analogy). [104]

With regards the **Qur'an**, Allah 🕮 says,

---

[103] Ibid. p.12.

[104] Ibn Taymiyyah has talked much about this subject in his book *"Iqtidaa' as-Siraat al-Mustaqeem"*, therefore, everything that I have written here is extracted from his book.

And those who do not witness *Az-Zur* [105]

Mujaahid said that the word "*Az-Zur*" (falsehood) means the festivals of the disbelievers, so did ar-Rabi' Ibn Anas, al-Qadee Abu Ya'laa and ad-Dhahaak. So, if Allah has announced that we should abandon witnessing these things; which after all, is only to be present, or to observe and listen, how then should we regard more active participation?

With regards to the **Sunnah**, Anas Ibn Maalik ﷺ related that: "When the Prophet ﷺ came to Madinah, the people had two days on which they engaged in games. He asked: "What about are these two days?" They said: "We used to engage ourselves on them in the pre-Islamic period". Then the Prophet ﷺ said, "Surely Allah has exchanged them for something better; the Day of the Sacrifice, and the Day of the Breaking of the Fast."[106]

Notice that the Messenger of Allah ﷺ did not approve of these celebrations, nor did he leave them to celebrate them, but said that Allah had exchanged them for something better; so the thing being exchanged is abandoned, and not added together. The word 'exchange' means 'replace', as in the verse:

Will you then take him (*Iblis*) and his offspring as protectors and helpers rather than Me,

---

[105] *Al-Furqan*: 72.
[106] "*Sunan Abu Dawud*", *The Book of Salat*, Hadith 1134, Ahmad, and an-Nasa'i; see: "*Iqtidaa' as-Siraat al-Mustaqeem*", p.184.

while they are enemies to you? What an evil is the exchange for wrong-doers [107]

The Prophet's words "for something better" proves that these two festivals were to replace those which people used to observe in the pre-Islamic period.

Also, We are warned against celebrating the festivals of the Jews and Christians, specifically, as we have been warned against resembling them, and have been told that we could, as a result of this, become part of their nations. This is a sterner warning than any with regard to the festivals of the pre-Islamic period. Indeed the religion of Ignorance presents no threat, and will not return before the final days of creation. Even if this were not the case, we would still be equally warned against them both. In any event, the threat of the enemy before you is always greater than that of the one who is absent and without authority. [108]

As for *Ijma'* (consensus), it is well known in history that the Jews, Christians, and Magians who settled to live among the Muslims that they continued to pay the *Jizyah* and celebrate their own festivals. Nevertheless, it was unknown for the Muslims of this time to celebrate any of these holidays with them. This was similar to Omar's policy specifically dealing with the non-Muslim communities within the Islamic State, which we will return to shortly. The Sahabah and the scholars

---

[107] *Al-Kahf* 50.
[108] *"Iqtidaa' as-Siraat al-Mustaqeem"*, p.184-186.

are in full agreement that non-Muslims are not permitted to publicly celebrate their festivals in a Muslim land. This being the case, how could the Muslims justify celebrating them for themselves? Is not worse than simple public celebration by the disbelievers alone?

Omar Ibn al-Khattab ؓ said, "Beware of their prattling gibberish, and that you should enter their churches on their holidays, for surely the Wrath of Allah descends upon them", this was reported by Abu as-Shaikh al-Asbahaanee and al-Bayhaqee with a 'Good *Isnad*.'

As for the **Qiyaas** position, the only legitimate holidays or festivals are those sanctioned by the Shari'ah. Allah ﷻ says:

To each among you, We have prescribed a law and a clear way [109]

There could be no distinction made between participating with the disbelievers in their festivals nor in the rest of their ways. To concur with them in their festivals is, in effect, to concur with them in their level of disbelief. To concur with one sect of theirs is to concur with part of a disbelieving people. Holidays are among the most prominent characteristics of a people's tradition, and the most visible of their acts of worship. To approve

---

[109] *Al-Ma'idah*: 48.

of such celebrations is to approve of the most central expressions of disbelief, and of its most visible rites. There is no doubt but that concurrence with this could eventually lead towards total disbelief.[110]

Finally, their celebrations are the most appalling things about them; approval of them is only approval of the very thing which could bring upon them the Wrath and Ire of Allah. What should also be considered is that a small concession turns to a broad license. Once a thing becomes familiar, then the masses could easily enter into it, forgetting its origin, until it becomes a part of their own tradition. Indeed, they may even come to take them for their own festivals, putting them finally on a par with the holy occasions ordained by Allah. This may continue to the point where it virtually supersedes their level of Islam, by raising up disbelief in its place.[111]

The disbelievers are heartened by the sight of Muslims celebrating at these occasions, with them. It brings them great joy to see what they proclaim raised up and in this way. Thus they achieve a small victory against the subjection which has befallen them at the hands of Muslims who once exacted from them tax and tribute.

In conclusion, we can say that imitating the disbelievers generally leads to disbelief or to sin. It is something which could not possibly be beneficial. This has been prohibited by the Shari'ah in all cases, whether the allurement to disbelief is plain or whether it is hidden.

---

[110] *"Iqtidaa' as-Siraat al-Mustaqeem"*, p. 208.
[111] Ibid. 209.

Having examined the situation with regard to festivals, in particular, and having understood its ruling, we should then apply what we have learned from the Qur'an and Sunnah. The modern festivals of the disbelievers and atheists, such as: May Day and Armistice Day, Christmas Day, Mothers' or Fathers' Day, Independence Day and the Lord Mayor's Show, etc, are all unsanctioned by Allah, and yet are put on the same level as the two festivals of Islam, and even seek to replace them. Muslims should not observe them and not acknowledge them, but rather should content ourselves with the two festivals of Islam, Eid al-Adha and Eid al-Fitr, and other days of celebration such as Friday and so on. This is enough to deflect from us the habits and desires of the disbelievers and their masters.

The Shining Example of Distinction of the First Muslim Society

Whenever discussion returns to the early days of the Muslim society, it takes on a special quality that warms the heart and inspires it with an admiration for these wonderful people, and this moves us to exert ourselves, for the sake of faith and guidance, to the common good.

Omar Ibn al-Khattab ؆ set a shining example of how to conduct relations between Muslims and non-Muslims, and in distinguishing the non-Muslim inhabitants of the Islamic state from the Muslims, in order to preserve a unique Islamic personality and to insure the rights of the non-Muslims which have been guaranteed by our faith. Omar's concern for this is itself an indication of the depth of his faith and the seriousness with which he viewed his responsibility to stewardship of this nation. It is a responsibility which he recognised well, as expressed in the Hadith, "All of you are shepherds and all of you are responsible for your flocks."[112]

The reason for choosing the example of the non-Muslim people (*Ahl adh-Dhimma*) living under the Islamic State is because of the special statue within the law. But the situation is different for the disbelievers who are at war with the Muslims or who oppose them openly. If non-Muslims are found in the heart of an Islamic society, then the Muslims should take special care that their contact with them does not lead to the adoption of their ways or customs; that the Islamic personality, which our religion itself raised up as a badge of distinction over all things, should not be watered down.

Furthermore, one of the qualities of this faith is justice, even with the disbelievers. But what are the limits and extent of this justice, especially with regard to non-Muslims who are permitted to live in the midst of an Islamic society? To answer this question we should return to the practice of Omar Ibn al-Khattab, whose

---

[112] "Sahih al-Bukhari", Vol.13/111, Hadith 7138, the Book of *Ahkaam*, and "Sahih Muslim", Vol.3/1459, Hadith 1829, the Book of *Ima'ra*.

concern was to preserve, at once, the integrity of the Muslims and the rights of the non-Muslims. This was known as *"Ash-Shurut al-Umariyyah"* (translated as Omar's Conditions). He decided that the non-Muslims, as well, should be distinguished from the Muslims in dress and appearance, in order that no Muslim would come to resemble them, and hence the Muslim identity would be lost.

Ibn Taymiyyah says that, in these Conditions, the point of distinguishing them from the Muslims, in terms of their dress and appearance, their names and even their modes of transport, was to separate them from the Muslims outwardly. Omar was not satisfied with simple distinction of beliefs, indeed he held that it included external appearance, as well. From this, Muslims are agreed that the disbelievers are to be clearly distinguishable, and that they should not come to resemble them. Omar Ibn al-Khattab, and Omar Ibn abdul-Aziz and others, returned to this theme frequently in order to make the point absolutely clear.

In addition, non-Muslims in an Islamic society must conceal whatever they do that is against the Shari'ah, as well as any overtly religious displays. They must not consume alcohol, openly, nor ring bells for their festivals and so on. We do not accept from them charity, but we take from them tribute as Allah has prescribed in His law.[113]

---

[113] *"Iqtidaa' as-Siraat al-Mustaqeem"*, p. 122-124.

Ibn al-Qayyim says in his book, *"Ahkaam Ahl adh-Dhimmah"* that Abdullah Ibn Ghanam said, "I wrote to Omar Ibn al-Khattab ﷺ about the matter of the Syrian Christians. He said that they were not permitted to build new churches, shrines, or communal structures, either in their towns or in the surrounding areas. Neither could they construct monasteries. What had fallen into ruin they were not to be rebuilt. He said that if any Muslim should arrive at one of their churches he should be given three days hospitality. They were prohibited from accommodating spies. They would not be allowed to conceal themselves from the Muslims, nor teach their children any of the Qur'an, nor make any display representing *'Shirk.'*

They would not prohibit any of their relations from embracing Islam, if they so wished, and that they should respect Muslims and to give up their places for those Muslims who wanted to sit. Their dress should not resemble that of the Muslims in any way, nor should they adopt their names, nor ride using saddles. They must not wear swords, sell alcohol, organise religious processions through the city, nor display the cross or anything of their scriptures in the streets of any Muslim quarter. Their funerals should not pass by Muslim homes and they would not raise their voices in mourning. They must not ring bells, even softly, they would not display palm fronds at Easter... If they diverged from any of these conditions they would no longer enjoy the protection of Muslims, and the Muslims would be permitted to treat them as they do any other of their enemies.[114]

---

[114] Ibn al-Qayyim, *"Ahkaam Ahl adh-Dhimma"*, Vol.2/661-662.

These Conditions have been related in another manner in other sources, but their meaning is nevertheless the same. For this reason Ibn al-Qayyim, commenting of the differing reports of it, said, "The fact that the conditions Omar laid down before *Ahl adh-Dhimmah* are so well known, adds more weight to them. The scholars accepted these reports as true, repeating them in their books, they supported them and continue to do so. The Khaliphs after him implemented them and enforced them."[115]

What an incredible difference there is between this pinnacle of faith and its pitiful example today, eking out his days on this Earth, groping and grovelling before the disbelief of the Westerners, or the champions in the East . Could such a person really consider himself to be a Muslim? Where is the grandeur, the power, the divine authority of the early generations of believers? Where has the feebleness, the servility, the obsequiousness of today's Muslims come from? Is it that the Muslims of today are *Dhimmis* to the disbelievers? It seems to me that even this assumption would be over optimistic. The Muslims today are even more powerless than the *Dhimmis* ever were. These people lived under a kind of subjugation, were stigmatised and knew certain restrictions, it is true. But the Muslims today are even more greatly subjugated, humiliated, and oppressed by their very submission to apostates in the East and disbelieves in the West; by their wonderment and awe

---

[115] Ibn al-Qayyim, *"Ahkaam Ahl adh-Dhimma"*, Vol.2/663, and *"Iqtidaa' as-Siraat al-Mustaqeem"*, p. 12.

before whatever the enemies of Islam may say; by their contempt and disdain for what the founders of our Ummah have left behind for us.

For this, Allah has cast them down in helplessness, in the international community; they are despised and ignored, and so they shall remain. As for the true Muslim, who is aware and is true to his faith, he should know where his place is, and who his true friends are. He must know that affection for the enemies of Allah, by allying himself to them, and imitating them, are all incompatible with faith. Rather those who do these things have but an empty claim on this religion. So much the worse for those who make such ludicrous claims.

The scholars have explained that, out of concern for the protection of the Muslims from any internal threats arising from the tolerant policy of Islam, the contract of the *Dhimmis* may be annulled under certain circumstances. Grounds for this are as follows:

(1) Aiding and abetting aggression against the Muslims, or the killing of a Muslim.

(2) Committing highway robbery against Muslims.

(3) Sheltering spies or spying on the Muslims, on behalf of the disbelievers.

(4) Adultery with Muslim women or illegally taking them as wives.

(5) Attempting to dissuade a Muslim from his religion.

(6) Insulting Allah or His Messenger ﷺ.[116]

The evidence for this last point, that their contract is annulled by insulting Allah or His Messenger, His Books or His Faith, and that the punishment for this is death, as it is for Muslims who do the same, is supported very strongly both in the **Qur'an** and the **Sunnah**, as well as by the **Consensus of the Sahabah**, the **Followers** and by **Qiyaas** (analogy).

As for the **Qur'anic** evidence, Allah ﷺ says,

But if they violate their oaths after their covenant, and attack your religion with disapproval and criticism, then fight the leaders of disbelief, for surely they have no binding oath, in order that they may desist[117]

And again,

Fight against those who believe not in Allah, nor in the Last Day, nor forbid that which has been forbidden by Allah and His Messenger and those who acknowledge not the religion of truth among the people of the Scripture, until they pay the *Jizyah* with willing submission, and feel themselves subdued[118]

---

[116] Ibn Taymiyyah, "*As-Saarimu al-Maslul Alaa Shaatim ar-Rasul*", p.5-26.
[117] *At-Taubah*: 12.
[118] *At-Taubah*: 29.

And finally, Allah ﷻ says,

> **Verily, those who annoy Allah and His Messenger, Allah has cursed them in the world and the Hereafter, and has prepared for them a humiliating torment. And those who annoy believing men and believing women undeservedly, they bear the crime of slander and manifest sin** [119]

As for the **Sunnah**, ash-Sha'abee relates that Ali ؓ said: "A Jewish woman used to abuse the Prophet ﷺ and disparage him. A man strangled her till she died. The Apostle of Allah ﷺ declared that no recompense was payable for her blood.." [120] (Narrated by Abu Dawud and Ibn Battah in his *Sunan*) The Hadith is *"Muttasil"* [*] since ash-Sha'abee had seen Ali, when the former was twenty years old. It could also be classed as *"Mursal"* [*], since ash-Sha'abee reported it in such a way as to imply that he had not heard it directly from Ali. In any event it is acceptable proof, since all *"Mursal"* Hadith reported by ash-Sha'abee are considered to be Sahih. [121]

---

[119] *Al-Ahzaab*: 57-58.

[120] "Sunan Abu Dawud", Vol.4/530, Hadith 4362, ad-Daaraqutni, Vol.3/112, Hadith 102.

[*] *Muttasil*: Continuous, a Hadith which has an uninterrupted *Isnad*.

[*] *Mursal*: a Hadith in which a man in the generation after the Companions quotes directly from the Prophet without mentioning the Companion from whom he received it.

[121] *"As-Saarimu al-Maslul Alaa Shaatim ar-Rasul"*, p.61.

Also, Ikrimah reported, on the authority of Ibn Abbas ⌖, that: "A blind man had a slave-mother who used to abuse the Prophet ⌖ and disparage him. He forbade her but she did not stop. He rebuked her but she did not give up her habit. One night she began to slander the Prophet ⌖ and abuse him. So he took a dagger, placed it on her belly, pressed it hard until it killed her. When the morning came, the Prophet ⌖ was informed about it. He assembled the people and said: I adjure by Allah the man who has done this action and I adjure him by my right to him that he should stand up. Jumping over the necks of the people and trembling the man stood up. He sat before the Prophet ⌖ and said: Apostle of Allah! I am her master; she used to abuse you and disparage you. I forbade her, but she did not stop, and I rebuked her, but she did not abandon her habit. I have two sons like pearls from her, and she was my companion. Last night she began to abuse and disparage you. So I took a dagger, put it on her belly and pressed it till I killed her. Thereupon the Prophet ⌖ said: O bear witness, no retaliation is payable for her blood."[122]

Other evidence from the Sunnah: Ash-Shafi'ee's argument that the *Dhimee* who insults the Prophet ⌖ should be killed; such a person is no longer protected by the law. Ash-Shafi'ee bases this on the killing of a Jew, Ka'ab Ibn al-Ashraf, an account of which appears in both al-Bukhari and Muslim.

---

[122] "Sunan Abu Dawud", Vol.4/528, Hadith 4361, an-Nasa'i', Vol.7/108. The *Isnad* of this Hadith is *Hasan*.

As for the **Consensus of Sahabah**, they have related many detailed reports supporting this position, which no one has denied. An example of this is an account concerning al-Muhajir Ibn Abee Umayyah, who was a governor of Yamamah and the surrounding area. It happened that there were two singers, one of whom had sung a song in which she insulted the Prophet ﷺ. Ibn Abu Umayyah cut off her hand and pulled out her two front teeth. The other woman sang ridiculing the Muslims, so he cut off her hand and removed her two front teeth as well. Later Abu Bakr ﷺ wrote to him saying, "I have got word about this woman who sang about the Prophet ﷺ and persisted in her insults. Had I known of this I would have ordered you to execute her. The statutes with regards to the Prophets are not like others. Any Muslim who engages in this sort of thing is an apostate, and any one at truce with us who does this has treacherously violated that truce."[123]

A man once came to Omar during his campaign in Syria, it was one of the People of the Book; his head had been split open and he had been badly beaten. Omar was furious when he saw this and sent for 'Awf Ibn Maalik al-Ashja'ee, since it was he who had done this to the man. When Omar asked him why, he said, "Ameer al-Mu'mineen, I saw him pursuing a Muslim woman riding a donkey. He poked her to make her fall but she did not fall, so he pushed her off and fell upon her molesting her." Omar said, "Bring the woman to me to confirm what you have said." So 'Awf came with her

---
[123] *"As-Saarimu al-Maslul Alaa Shaatim ar-Rasul"*, p.200.

father and her husband who told Omar the same thing that 'Awf had said. Then Omar ordered that the Jew be crucified. He told him, "We did not make peace with you so that you should behave like this." Then he turned to those present and said, "Be mindful of your duty to Allah, under the protection of Muhammad ﷺ. Whoever among you does as this man has done will have no protection."[124]

As for **Qiyaas**, we find several aspects[125]:

One is that slandering our faith and insulting our Prophet ﷺ is aggression against us and an act of war. It is a violation that invalidates the truce between us and our enemies, and is no different from any other assault against us.

The second point is that our agreements with the disbelievers are conditional, upon their leaving off openly abusing our religion and maligning our Prophet, in the same way as it is conditional upon their leaving off killing the Muslims and waging war against them.

The third point is that Allah requires of us both support for and reverence towards His Prophet. To support him is to help and protect him. Reverence towards him means that we glorify and honour him; this entails defending him by whatever means are necessary.

---

[124] Abu Ubaid, "*Al-Amwaal*", p.235-236.
[125] "*As-Saarimu al-Maslul Alaa Shaatim ar-Rasul*", p.206-209.

We are under no obligation to make peace with the *Dhimmis* while they indulge in defaming our Prophet openly, since if we were to tolerate this from them, we would be abandoning our obligations with respect to Allah's messenger ﷺ.

Places which The Enemies of Allah are Forbidden from Entering and Living In

Allah ﷻ has said,

> **O you who believe! Verily, the idolaters are *Najasun* (impure). So let them not come near *Al-Masjid al-Haram* after this year. And if you fear poverty, Allah will enrich you of His bounty if He will. Surely, Allah is All-Knowing, All-Wise** [126]

Abu Hurayrah ﷺ said, "While we were in the mosque, Allah's Apostle came out to us and said, "Let us proceed to the Jews." So we went along with him till we reached Bait-al-Midras (a place where the Torah used to be recited and all the Jews of the town used to gather). The Prophet ﷺ stood up and addressed them, "O Assembly of Jews! Embrace Islam and you will be safe!" The Jews replied, "O Aba-l-Qasim! You have conveyed Allah's Message to us." The Prophet ﷺ said, "That is

---

[126] *At-Taubah*: 28.

118

what I want (from you)." He repeated his first statement for the second time, and they said, "You have conveyed Allah's Message, O Aba-l-Qasim." Then he said it for the third time and added, "You should know that the earth belongs to Allah and His Messenger, and I want to exile you from this land, so whoever among you owns some property, can sell it, otherwise you should know that the Earth belongs to Allah and His Messenger." This is reported by Muslim and Al-Bukhari. This wording is from Al-Bukhari.[127]

The Prophet ﷺ also said, "Expel the idolaters (*Mushrikeen*) from the Arabian peninsula."[128] He ﷺ said: "I will expel the Jews and Christians from the Arabian Peninsula and will not leave any, but Muslims."[129]

These clear and unambiguous texts, and others, illustrate quite plainly the extent to which Islam is concerned about the protection of the nation from disbelieving communities, and from political coexistence with them which may cause the Muslims to take them for friends and protectors, a thing which Allah has forbidden them from doing.

Ash-Sha'fi'i, may Allah have Mercy upon him, said: "They are prohibited (from entering) the Hijaz. That

---

[127] "Sahih al-Bukhari", vol.12/317, Hadith 6944, and "Sahih Muslim", Vol.3/1387, Hadith 1765.
[128] "Sahih al-Bukhari", vol.6/170, Hadith 3053, and "Sahih Muslim", Vol.3/1258, Hadith 1637.
[129] "Sahih Muslim", Vol.3/1388, Hadith 1767.

is to say Makkah, Madinah, Yamaamah and their respective hinterlands. As for those parts of the Hijaz lying outside the two Harams (of Makkah and Madinah), while those of the People of the Book, and others, are prohibited from either settling or taking up residence therein, they may, nevertheless, with the permission of the Imam, enter for the accomplishment of some mission which is in the interests of the Muslims. Such as the delivery of a letter, or the delivery of goods of which the Muslims are in need. But even if they do enter for purposes of trade, one would still be in little need of them. They are permitted to do this so long as they surrender a portion of their trade, though they may not remain for more than three (days)."[130]

Ibnu al-Qayyim, may Allah have Mercy upon him, comments on these words of ash-Sha'fi'i saying, "As for the *Haram* of Makkah, they (the disbelievers) are completely prohibited from entering its precincts. Were they to send an emissary it would not be permitted for the Imam to grant any of them entry. In this case a Secretary, or some other appointed person, would be sent to meet him (outside the Holy Precincts). With regard to the *Haram* of Madinah they are not prohibited from entering it in order to deliver a letter, engage in commerce, or deliver goods."[131]

---

[130] Ibn al-Qayyim, *"Ahkaam Ahl adh-Dhimma"*, Vol.1/184, and Abu Ubaid's *"Al-Amwaal"*, p.90.
[131] *"Ahkaam Ahl adh-Dhimma"*, Vol.1/185.

Response to some Objections

Some people say that Allah ﷻ has prohibited the pagans from approaching the *Haram* of Makkah, but not the People of the Book. They cite the announcement of the Prophet ﷺ, on the day of the Greater Hajj, when he said, "After this year no pagan shall be permitted to join the pilgrimage." They say that these pagans who used to perform the Hajj were idolaters, not People of the Book. There are two points about the entry of the People of the Book into the Holy Precincts, and about the word "pagan" (*Mushrik*). According to Ibn Omar ﷺ and others the People of the Book are indeed pagans. Abdullah ibn Omar used to say, "I do not know of a greater *Shirk* than to say that the Messiah is the son of Allah, or that Ezra is the son of Allah. For Allah has said,

They (Jews and Christians) took their rabbis and their priests as lords besides Allah, and the Messiah, son of Mary, while they were commanded only to worship none but One God, none has the right to be worshipped but He. Praise and Glory be to Him, from having the partners they associate with Him[132]

The second point about the command, "they shall not enter" concerns the word "pagan," for Allah has set the People of the Book apart from the pagans, saying,

---

[132] *At-Taubah*: 31.

121

Verily! Those who believe and those who are Jews, and Christians, and Sabians [133]

Ibn Taymiyyah comments, "The fact of the matter is that the origin of their religion is *Tawhid*, so they are not, at least originally, pagans. But *Shirk* is new to them and so they are pagans by virtue of this, rather than by virtue of the origin of their faith. Supposing that the People of the Book are not included amongst the pagans with reference to this verse (2:62), they are included amongst them in terms of the general meaning of the term, that is, that they are "impure". This establishes the ruling that is to be applied generally.

All of the Sahabah and the scholars understood the verse: ❨**So let them not come near *Al-Masjid al-Haram* after this year**❩, as referring to all of Makkah and the Holy Precincts. None of them thought that this referred only to the Mosque itself around which the Tawaaf is performed. When this verse was revealed, the Jews were still living at Khaibar and they were not subsequently banned from entering Madinah."[134]

---

[133] *Al-Baqarah*: 62.
[134] "*Ahkaam Ahl adh-Dhimmah*", Vol.1/189.

CHAPTER SEVEN: Muslims Dealing with Non-Muslims

Section One: Difference between Alliance and Courtesy

A word about the so-called inter-faith movement

It is necessary at this point to correct a common misunderstanding: Someone like myself, at the beginning of his studies, may be astonished to see great scholars 'become ensnared by the enemies of Islam: the Christians and the Jews'. One fears that the friendship of non-Muslims will blur a Muslim's identity and distort his personality.

It is worth pointing out, from the beginning, that whereas every Messenger was sent by Allah to call his people to the worship of Allah alone, the differences in the laws revealed to them are a matter of Divine Wisdom and beyond our limited comprehension; Allah ﷻ says:

> **And verily, We have sent among every nation a Messenger, (proclaiming): Worship Allah and avoid *Taghut* [1]**

Nevertheless, every revelation that preceded Islam was transformed by the corrupting hand of man;

---

[1] *An-Nahl*: 36.

Woe to those who write the Book with their own hands and then say, 'This is from Allah,' that they may purchase a small gain therewith. Woe to them for what their hands have written, and woe to them for that they earn thereby [2]

Because of this Muhammad Ibn Abdullah ﷺ was sent with the final revelation to mankind, wiping away all the law revealed before it. However, it is very important to look at some of the claims made in favour of the so-called inter-faith movement, which, according to those who support it, is not merely in the interests of Islam but indeed of all humanity.

Sheikh Mustafa al-Muraaghee said, in an address he delivered to the World Faith Congress, "Islam has eradicated religious bigotry from the hearts of the Muslims, banished all hatred towards the followers of the other Semitic faiths and ordained a universal brotherhood of man. There is nothing to prevent people of all faiths from living side by side." [3]

Shaikh Muhammad Abu Zahrah said, "If faiths differ then let each call others to his own, with wisdom and exhortation, leave aside the fanaticism that poisons

---

[2] *Al-Baqarah*: 79.
[3] Dr. Wahbah az-Zuhayli, "*Athaar al-Harb Fi al-Fiqh al-Islami*", p.63, 2nd edition, 1385 A.H.

truth, and abandon compulsion or coercion in the absence of evidence or proof..″[4]

Dr. Wahbah az-Zuhayli asserts that, "It is not the aim of Islam to impose itself on mankind as the single world faith. Such an attempt must surely end in failure, since it flies in the face of reality and contradicts Divine Will."[5]

There are many more examples of this. It is clear that these and others like them are the true heirs of their great master Jamaal ad-Deen al-Afghanee, who was himself under the influence of the Masons. Indeed, al-Afghanee was the first to raise the call for a fraternity of faiths, stating in a document entitled, "The Theory of Unity", "I discovered after much examination, enquiry and careful study that the three monotheistic religions are in complete agreement both in terms of principles and in terms of aims. If any one of them is lacking in any measure of good, another of them compensates for this deficiency...as a result of this, there appeared to me a great hope that the followers of these three faiths could be drawn together, as faith itself is a single jewel with a single source and aim. Towards this goal that mankind had taken, in the course of this short life, a great step was made towards peace. So my ideas began to take shape, the lines were drawn and pages became black with ink as I raised this call. But I did not mix with the communities of all faiths, and neither did I search deeply into the reasons for the differences among the people of a single

---

[4] *"Al-Alaaqaat ad-Dawliyyah Fi al-Islam"*, p.42, 1384 A.H.
[5] *"Athaar al-Harb Fi al-Fiqh al-Islami"*, p.65.

religion and their division into groups, factions and parties..."[6]

Of course, anyone will be able to see the error of these words. The claim is that Islam permits the Christian to call others to his faith, the Jews to invite others to Judaism, the Buddhists to spread Buddhism, and so on, for whatever religions people may have invented; or whatever faiths they may have twisted or perverted. Are those who raise this call really ignorant of the Quranic account of the Children of Israel, of how they killed the Prophets and twisted the message of the Torah and the Gospel, of how they tampered with the Books revealed to them, finally filling them with the fruit of their own desires? Can these people really be unaware of the words of Allah,

> **Surely, disbelievers are those who said: "Allah is the third of the three."** [7]

And of the words of the Most High,

> **And the Jews say: Ezra is the son of Allah, and the Christians say: Messiah is the son of Allah. That is their saying with their mouths. They imitate the saying of those who disbelieved of old. Allah's Curse be on them, how they are deluded away from the truth!** [8]

---

[6] Abdul Aziz Sayyid al-Ahl, *"Khaatiraat Jamaal ad-Deen al-Afghanee"*, p.14, and p.158.

[7] *Al-Ma'idah*: 73.

[8] *At-Taubah*: 30.

And He ﷻ said,

> They wish that you reject Faith, as they have rejected (Faith), and that you all become equal (like one another) [9]

And,

> Many of the People of the Scripture wish that if they could turn you away as disbelievers, after you have believed [10]

These are only a few of the many verses which explain the enmity of the People of the Book for the Muslims. May Allah have Mercy upon Sayyidd Qutb who pointed out, "While the tolerance of Islam for the People of the Book is one thing, taking them for friends and guardians is quite another. These two aspects sometimes confuse Muslims who do not have a clear picture in their own souls of the sublime truth of this faith, nor of its mission, the goal of which is to spread it on earth, according to the image of Islam which is different, in nature, from all other concepts known to humanity.

Those who remain confused about this truth are also lacking in a sense of devotion to the truth of the Creed, as they are lacking in awareness and knowledge of the true nature of the People of the Book and of the conflict with them. They do not understand the clear and

---

[9] *An-Nisa'*: 89.
[10] *Al-Baqarah*: 109.

simple Quranic position, with regard to the People of the Book, since they confuse the call of Islam to tolerance; participation with, and respect for these communities - within the context of the Muslim society in which they live - with the principle of alliance, which can only be sealed with Allah, His messenger, and with the Muslim society at large. They forget the clear statement of the Qur'an that the People of the Book are allies to one another in their struggle against the Muslim community, and that this is a part of their nature. They forget that these people are full of hatred for the Muslims, because of their Islam, that they will never be happy with any Muslim until he abandons his religion and follows theirs.

It is the height of naivety and foolishness to suspect that we share a common road with the People of the Book, a road which we should follow for the sake of the Deen; to stand side by side, in the face of disbelief and atheism, for they are themselves with the disbelievers and atheists, whenever either of these rise up against the Muslims.

The simple minded may say, "Surely we will be able to join hands with the People of the Book against secularism and atheism, since we are all people of religion!" They forget completely the lessons of the Qur'an, just as much as they forget the lessons of history. It was, after all, the People of the Book who used to say to the disbelievers from among the pagans,

These are more rightly guided than those who believe [11]

It was they who incited the pagans to attack the Muslims at Madinah and who were their cloak and their shield. It was the People of the Book who pursued with the Crusades for two hundred years, it was they who mounted the Inquisition in Spain, and it was they who drove away the Palestinians and moved the Jews in after them, with the help and co-operation of humanists and secularists.

It is the People of the Book who make war on the Muslims in every land, from Ethiopia, to Somalia and Eritrea, and across the world; they work hand in hand with the forces of humanism, secularism, and base materialism; in Yugoslavia, in China and Turkestan, in India and in every land!

Those who imagine - in their wild fantasies - that there could ever be between us and the People of the Book any kind of alliance or mutual defence of religion against the secular and atheistic humanist assault, could not have read the Qur'an. Or, if they have, must then confuse the tolerance shown to the disbelievers, which is the hallmark of Islam, with alliance with them, which the Qur'an takes pains to warn us about. Then they attempt to explain away the clear distinction which exists between the Muslims and the People of the Book, basing their arguments upon the tolerance of Islam and the close historical relationships among the people of the Semitic

---

[11] *An-Nisa'*: 51.

faiths. Just as they are mistaken in their understanding of the nature of these faiths, so they are mistaken about the real meaning of tolerance.

The religion which was revealed to the Messenger of Allah ﷺ is the Religion of Allah. As for tolerance, it is a matter of human relations, and it does not enter into the domain of correct belief or social organisation. As for those who misunderstand these things, they attempt to play down the absolute certainty which must be in the soul of every Muslim; that Allah does not accept any other religion than Islam. Indeed, it is the obligation of every Muslim to apply the lessons which Allah has taught us, in Islam, to his own life and to reject any attempt to replace this with anything less than it, or anything which would claim to be equal to it - however insignificant it may be. Allah ﷺ says:

> **Truly, the religion in the Sight of Allah is Islam** [12]

And

> **And whoever seeks a religion other than Islam, it will never be accepted from him** [13]

In fact, Islam was revealed to correct the beliefs of the People of the Book, as it was also sent to correct the beliefs of the pagans. They were all called to Islam, which is 'The True Religion'; no other faith than this will be accepted, from anyone. The Muslim is obliged to call

---

[12] *Al-Imran*: 19.
[13] *Al-Imran*: 85.

the People of the Book to Islam, just as he is obliged to
call humanists and pagans alike to it. No Muslim may be
permitted to force anyone, whether People of the Book or
not, to accept Islam; since faith cannot be forced into the
heart. Coercion in religion is prohibited by Islam, and
what is prohibited by Islam could never bear fruit."[14]

---

[14] Sayyid Qutb: "*Fi Dhilal al-Qur'an*", Vol.2/909-915.

Difference between Alliance and Courtesy

We have mentioned above that Alliance is one thing and courtesy is another. This position is based upon the words of Allah, Who says,

Allah does not forbid you to deal justly and kindly with those who fought not against you on account of religion and did not drive you out from your homes. Verily, Allah loves those who deal with equity [15]

Scholars have not agreed about the interpretation of this verse. While some of them, such as Mujahid, have said that it refers to those who believed and remained in Makkah and did not join the *Hijrah*. Thus Allah instructs the Believers to treat them with kindness and respect. Others maintain that it refers to people other than those of Makkah who did not join the *Hijrah*. Still others say that it refers to the pagans of Makkah who had neither fought the Muslims nor persecuted them, but that Allah later instructed them to fight them, cancelling the former command and issuing a new one. This was the position of Qatadah.

Ibn Jarir at-Tabari's view of this is that the strongest position belongs to those who say that Allah has not prevented us from good conduct with any people, regardless of their nation or their faith, who do not

---

[15] *Al-Mumtahinah*: 8.

struggle against us; nor should we disregard their rights or fail to deal with them justly. This is because Allah, Glorious and Mighty is He, refers to them generally as, **❨Those who fought not against you on account of religion and did not drive you out from your homes❩**, thus gathering together all those who share this quality of non-aggression, with no further distinction being made among them. Whoever says that this verse has been cancelled by some later part of the Revelation is mistaken. Indeed, courtesy and respect are required of a Believer towards any of the 'people of war'; those who are relatives and those who are not. So long as they do not hinder the Muslims, assault them or take up arms against them, their position is assured.

This is illustrated by the story of 'Asma and her mother which was related by Ibn Zubayr.[16] Islam is like this in practice, even in times of dispute; it preserves the roots of affection in the heart of the believer, by means of correct conduct and fairness, in anticipation of the day when his opponent must be silenced, in the knowledge that goodness means a place in the shadow of Allah's High Banner.[17]

We have already discussed the position with regard to familial ties with disbelieving relatives and pointed out that this does not in any way imply alliance with them. This point is made even more clear by the story of 'Asma bint Abu Bakr, may Allah be pleased with her, and her mother. Both Al-Bukhari and Muslim

---

[16] *"Tafsir at-Tabari"*, Vol.28/66.
[17] Sayyid Qutb: *"Fi Dhilal al-Qur'an"*, Vol.6/3544.

reported that 'Asma narrated, "My mother, who was a pagan, had come to see me in the days of the Messenger of Allah ﷺ, so I sought the advice of the Prophet ﷺ about her visit. I told him, 'My mother has come to see me and she is outside Islam, shall I treat her kindly?' He said, 'Yes, treat your mother kindly."[18]

Al-Khattabi explained this Hadith: "A disbelieving mother should be treated kindly just as a Muslim mother, and the disbelieving parents should be supported even if their son is a Muslim."[19]

Ibn Hajar points out that to keep up family ties and behave well with relatives does not mean that you should have for them the same love and affection that Allah has forbidden to the Muslims saying,

You will not find any people who believe in Allah and the Last Day, making friendship with those who oppose Allah and His Messenger [20]

There is a difference between those who fight and those who do not.[21]

---

[18] "Sahih al-Bukhari", Vol.5/233, Hadith 2620, and "Sahih Muslim", Vol.2/696, Hadith 1003.
[19] *"Fath al-Bari"*, Vol.5/234.
[20] *Al-Mujadilah*: 22.
[21] *"Fath al-Bari"*, Vol.5/233.

According to Ibn al-Qayyim: "The obligation to maintain family ties and support, even in the face of difference over religion, is established by the verse,

And We have enjoined upon man (to be dutiful and good) to his parents - His mother carried him in weakness upon weakness, and his weaning is in two years - Give thanks to Me and to your parents. To Me is the final destination. But if they strive with you to make you join in worship with Me others that of which you have no knowledge, then obey them not, but behave with them in the world kindly [22]

To abandon your mother and your father is both immoral and unjust, whether you are rich or whether you are poor. In fact, Allah has required us to honour family ties and has condemned whoever cuts them off,

And be careful of your duty toward Allah in Whom you demand your mutual rights, and (do not cut the relations of) the wombs (kinship) [23]

And finally there is the Hadith saying, "No one who cuts off relations with his family shall enter Paradise."[24]

---

[22] *Luqman*: 14-15.

[23] *An-Nisa'*: 1.

[24] "Sahih al-Bukhari", Vol.10/415, Hadith 5984, and "Sahih Muslim", Vol.4/1981, Hadith 2556.

It is obligatory to respect the family bond, even with disbelievers, everyone may choose his own faith. The analogy drawn between the family bond and inheritance is not a valid one, since inheritance rights rest, in principle, upon personal loyalty to custom and tradition, whereas the family bond is ultimately a matter of honouring one's personal responsibilities and obligations towards one's relatives.

Allah has granted rights to close relatives, even if they are disbelievers. Disbelief does not negate such rights, in this world. Allah ﷻ has said:

Worship Allah and join none with Him in worship, and do good to parents, kinsfolk, orphans, the poor who beg, the neighbour who is near of kin, the neighbour who is not of kin, the companion by your side, the wayfarer and (the slaves) whom your right hands possess. Verily, Allah does not like such as are proud and boastful [25]

Everyone mentioned in this verse has his right, which should not be denied him, even though he may be a disbeliever. So how could we deny our relatives this courtesy, which Allah has required of us, while observing the same towards others?[26]

Therefore, it becomes clear to us that association founded upon affection and support is one thing, and

---

[25] *An-Nisa'*: 36.
[26] *"Ahkaam Ahl adh-Dhimma"*, Vol.2/417-418.

family bonds and courtesy towards disbelieving relatives is clearly another. Lastly, the tolerance of Islam is further demonstrated by the way prisoners, elderly men and women, and children are treated in war, as is known from its shining history.

Section Two: Dealing with Disbelievers

Trading

Ibn Taymiyyah said: "The principle is: people are allowed to do whatever they need to do, so long as this has neither been prohibited by the Qur'an nor Sunnah. This same principle applies inversely to acts of worship; by which one intends to draw near to Allah: such acts are invalid without authority from either of these sources. The aim of worship is only to draw near to Allah. For religion is what Allah has sanctioned, and the prohibited is what Allah has forbidden; in contradiction to those whom Allah has condemned, who forbade things which He had not forbidden, associated partners with Him without any instruction, and invented acts of worship without His Authority."[27]

Starting from this rule, and relying upon the text of the Qur'an, the Sunnah, the practice of the Prophet ﷺ, his Companions and the Imams of the Ummah, we can say, dealings with the disbelievers for purposes of trade and so on cannot be considered evidence of alliance. In fact, trade with them is allowed. When Ibn Taymiyyah was asked about trade with the Mongols he said, "Whatever trade is allowed with others is also allowed with Mongols. That which is not allowed with others is not allowed with Mongols. You may buy goods they produce, horses and so on from them, just as you may buy such things from Bedouins, Turks or Kurds. You

---

[27] "*As-Siyaasah ash-Shar'iyyah*", p.155.

may likewise sell them food, clothing and such things as you are allowed to sell to others.

As for selling to them, or to anyone else, things that they will misuse, such as arms or horses in order to make war illegally, this is clearly not allowed. Allah has said,

> **Help one another to righteousness and pious duty; but do not help one another to sin and transgression** [28]

If they, or others, offer goods for sale, which they have illegally taken from someone else, then you should not buy them except in order to restore them to their rightful owner. If you buy them for this purpose and are then unable to find the person they belong to, then you must use them for the benefit of the Muslims. If you know that the goods they offer for sale include stolen goods but you do not know which are stolen and which not, then this does not prevent you from trading with them, just as you may shop in a market even where you know stolen goods are sold."[29]

Al-Bukhari reported in "The Book of Sales", in the Chapter 'Buying and selling with pagans and with the enemy at war', a Hadith quoting Abdur-Rahman Ibn Abi Bakr ؋ who said, "We were with the Prophet ﷺ when a tall pagan with long matted unkempt hair came forwar, ddriving his sheep. The Prophet ﷺ asked him, 'Are those

---

[28] *Al-Ma'idah*: 2.
[29] *"Al-Masa'il al-Maardiniyyah"*, p.132-133.
.

139

sheep for sale or gifts?' The pagan replied, 'They are for sale.' So the Prophet ﷺ bought one sheep from him."[30]

Ibn Bataal said, "Trade with the disbelievers is permitted, but you cannot sell things to people at war with the Muslims, thereby helping them against the Muslims."[31]

It is confirmed that the Prophet ﷺ had taken thirty *wasaq*[*] of barley from a Jew, leaving his coat of mail as mortgage.[32] Ibn Taymiyyah also says that: "If a man goes to '*Dar al-Harb*' for trade we have no objection to it, since Abu Bakr ؓ went to conduct business in Syria, in the days of the Prophet ﷺ, when it was still '*Dar al-Harb*'. There are other similar accounts to this... If a Muslim sells the disbelievers food and clothing, incense and such things for the celebration of their festivals, or gives these to them, then we consider this to be a kind of assistance to them in organising their festivals, which are forbidden. The grounds for this decision are that it is not permitted even to sell either grapes or grape juice to them so that they could make wine. Likewise one is not allowed to sell them weapons with which they could attack Muslims."[33]

---

[30] "Sahih al-Bukhari", Vol.4/410, Hadith 2216.

[31] *"Fath al-Bari"*, Vol.4/410.

[*] *Wasaq*: A *Wasaq* is sixty *Saa'*, a *Saa'* is four *Mudd*, a *Mudd* is one and one third *Ratl*, a *Ratl* is four scooped handfuls: what a man can hold in both hands cupped, fills them but does not overflow from them. These are measures of volume rather than weight.

[32] *"Musnad Ahmad"*, Vol.5/137, Hadith 3409, Ahmad Shakir said its *Isnad* is Good.

[33] *"Iqtidaa' as-Siraat al-Mustaqeem"*, p. 229.

Waqf (Endowment Fund)

Ibn al-Qayyim said, "If the disbelievers donate something for a charitable purpose, it should be considered, for if they endow something (as *Waqf*) to a person or a group, such as: supporting the poor and needy, repairing roads and public services, or assisting their children, such an endowment is correct; their rights in respect to these things are no different from those of Muslims. But, if one of them then demands that his children or relatives should be allowed to remain in their disbelief as a condition of this support, saying, 'If any of you become Muslims then you will get nothing', then, as such a condition is illegal, his right to such assistance would cease. The Caliph should not agree to such conditions, as it is anti-Islamic and contradictory to the revelation Allah sent His Messenger with.

As for Muslims' endowment to them, this is allowed, so long as it conforms to the Shari'ah in every respect. Thus Muslims can assist them or their relatives, as state of belief is not taken into consideration when receiving help, so it does not stop a disbeliever from being helped. So if a Muslim supports his son, father or other relatives, it is their right to receive this support, even if they remain in disbelief. But if they become Muslims, then their right to this is even greater.

Having an endowment fund (*Waqf*) for their churches, synagogues and places of religious gathering,

---

* *Waqf*: also *Habus*, an unalianable endowment for a charitable purpose which cannot be given away or sold to anyone else.

141

where they celebrate their festivals and practice distorted ritual beliefs, is neither accepted from the Muslims nor the disbelievers. This is because it only supports and encourages disbelief and is, in the view of Islam, prohibited."[34]

Visiting their Sick and Greeting them on Festivals

On the authority of Anas ⌖, Al-Bukhari narrated in "The Book of Funerals": "When a Jewish boy, who used to serve the Prophet ⌖, became ill the Prophet ⌖ went to call on him. He sat near the head of his bed and told him, 'Accept Islam'. He looked at his father who was standing nearby. His father said, 'Do as Abu al-Qaasim says'. So he accepted Islam. As he left the Prophet ⌖ said, 'Praise be to Allah who has saved him from Hell Fire.'"[35]

Al-Bukhari also related the story of the Prophet's encouragement of Abu Taalib, at the time of his death, to accept Islam.[36]

Ibn Bataal says that visiting the sick should be in order to encourage them to enter Islam, if this is not the reason for visiting them, then it is not allowed.[37] Ibn Hajar remarks that whether or not visiting them is

---

[34] "Ahkaam Ahl adh-Dhimma", Vol.1/299-302, and "Majmu'at ar-Rasaail wal-Masa'il", Vol.1/229.
[35] "Sahih al-Bukhari", Vol.3/219, Hadith 1356.
[36] "Sahih al-Bukhari", Vol.3/222, Hadith 1360.
[37] "Fath al-Bari", Vol.10/119.

allowed depends on the intentions for going, since there may well be other hidden benefits from visiting the sick.[38]

As for wishing them well, on their holidays and festivals of distorted belief, everyone agrees that this is not allowed. This includes telling them 'Merry Christmas,' or 'Happy Easter,' or 'Happy Hanukkah,' and so forth, since this is really congratulating them in their states of disbelief, which is forbidden. It is like wishing them well for the worship of Christ, indeed, it is worse than this before Allah, and more loathsome than wishing them good health as they drink alcoholic drinks; worse than killing someone unjustly or engaging in illicit sex.

A lot of people who do not cherish their faith fall into this trap, not knowing the seriousness of what they do. Whoever wishes a man well in his transgression, his *Bidah* or disbelief has exposed himself to the Wrath of Allah. God fearing and pious people, from among those of knowledge, used to avoid greeting local rulers, foolish 'Lords' and 'Professors' and so forth, to stay well clear of Allah's Wrath. 'If a man had the misfortune of seeing one of them he would busy himself to shield himself from any trouble that might arise from their presence. He would approach them without praising them nor wishing them well in their wrong ways, but speak to them civilly; there is no harm in this.[39]

---

[38] Ibid.
[39] *"Ahkaam Ahl adh-Dhimma"*, Vol.1/205-206.

This raises the question of calling them by honorific titles like sir or master which is certainly forbidden. Evidence for this is to be found in a *Marfu'* [*] Hadith saying: "Do not say, 'Master' to a hypocrite for if you take him for 'Master', then you have annoyed your Lord, Glorious and Exalted."[40]

It is likewise forbidden, as Ibn al-Qayyim points out, to give them official titles of respect or state honours, and if they adopt these names themselves; Muslims may not call them by these names such as Muiz ad-Dawlah, ar-Rasheed, etc.. If he is a Christian then you should refer to him as 'Christian', or Crusader' and to the Jew you say 'Jew'. Then Ibn al-Qayyim continues, "But today we see them sitting in official committees. People stand for them greeting them warmly. They are given responsibility over military requisitions, and the treasury. They are called such things Abu al-'Alaa', Abu al-Fadl and Abu at-Tayyib, they are called Hassan, Uthman and Ali! Yet their names used to be John, Matthew and George, Paul, Ezra, Erazmus and Ezeikel. In every age they have positions in the state and men of public life."[41]

This is what Ibn al-Qayyim had to say about it, and he died six hundred and fifty years ago. But you see the Muslims today who are like the foam on the sea. They assert that they are Muslims, but follow the

---

[*] *Marfu'*: "Elevated", a narration from the Prophet 鐢 mentioned by a Companion, e.g. 'The Prophet 鐢 said…'.
[40] "Sunan Abu Dawud", Vol.5/257, Hadith 4977, Albani said its *Isnad* is Sahih.
[41] "*Ahkaam Ahl adh-Dhimma*", Vol.2/771.

enemies of Allah in all things, large and small. If one of the disbelievers were to enter a lizard's hole, they would follow after them. They do not simply follow them, but they do it to unbelievable extremes. At every opportunity our enemies are congratulated, well-wishes are sent, toasts made to their health, and heartfelt honey-sweet greetings are conveyed!

Greeting Disbelievers in the Street

The scholars have not agreed about the significance of Allah's statement regarding Ibrahim ﷺ when he called his father to Islam, even though his father refused, Ibrahim said to him ❨**Salaamun 'alayka**❩, (Translated as: **Peace be on you**) (19:48). The majority say that this is not a greeting but a conciliation. At-Tabari says that it means 'you have my assurance or my trust'. Because of this, you should not greet a disbeliever before he greets you.[42] Others, however, have said that it is a farewell greeting and so have permitted extending greetings to disbelievers, even if you are the first to do so. Someone asked Ibn Uyaynah, "Are we allowed to greet the disbelievers?" He said, 'Yes. Allah has said,

Allah does not forbid you to deal justly and kindly with those who fought not against you on account of religion and drove you not out from your homes [43]

---

[42] *"Tafsir al-Qurtubi"*, Vol.11/111-112.
[43] *Al-Mumtahinah*: 8.

And also He said,

Indeed there has been an excellent example for you in Ibrahim [44]

And Ibrahim said to his father: 《*Salaamun 'alayka*》. Al-Qurtubi said that the most obvious thing about this verse is what Sufyan Ibn Uyaynah had said about it.

There are two views about it. According to a report from Abu Hurayrah, the Prophet ﷺ said: "Do not salute the Jews and Christians first, and when you meet them on the road, force them to go to the narrowest part of it." [45]

It is reported in both Sahih al-Bukhari and Sahih Muslim, on the authority of Usamah Ibn Zaid, who said, "The Prophet ﷺ rode on a donkey, with a saddle underneath which there was a thick soft Fadakiya velvet sheet. Usamah Ibn Zaid was his companion rider, and he was going to pay a visit to Sa'd bin Ubadah (who was sick) at the dwelling place of Bani Al-Harith bin Al-Khazraj; this incident happened before the battle of Badr. The Prophet ﷺ passed by a gathering in which there were Muslims, pagan idolators and Jews, and among them there was 'Abdullah Ibn Ubay Ibn Salul and Abdullah Ibn Rawahah. Then a cloud of dust raised by the animal covered that gathering, 'Abdullah Ibn Ubay covered his nose with his Rida (sheet) and said (to the Prophet ﷺ),

---

[44] *Al-Mumtahinah*: 4.
[45] "Sahih Muslim", Vol.4/1707, Hadith, the Book of as-Salam, and Abu Dawud, Vol.5/384, Hadith 5205.

146

"Don't cover us with dust." The Prophet greeted them."[46] (the Hadith)

Al-Qurtubi remarks, "The first Hadith indicates that we should not greet them first since this is a mark of respect and this is not fitting for disbelievers; however, the second Hadith permits us to do so." At-Tabari said, "Usamah's account does not contradict the report of Abu Hurayrah, neither does the one diverge from the other. Abu Hurayrah's report illustrates the general rule, while Usamah's account indicates the exception. An-Nakha'ee said, "If you have some business with a Jew or a Christian, then greet him first."

The meaning of Abu Hurayrah's account "Do not salute the Jews and Christians first", is then further qualified with, 'if you don't have any reason to do so.' That is, if you have no pressing need of them or business with them, and if it is a friend, a neighbour or a traveller, whose right is it that you should greet him. At- Tabari adds, "It has been related that the Salaf used to greet the People of the Book. Thus, Ibn Mas'ud greeted a head-man, whom he accompanied on his journey. 'Alqamah then asked him, "Abu Abdur-Rahman, is it not abominable to greet them first?" Ibn Mas'ud said, "Yes, but it is also the right of companionship."

Al-Awzaa'ee said, "If you greet them, then better men than you have also done so, but if you do not greet them, better men than you have done this before." Hassan

---

[46] "Sahih al-Bukhari", Vol.11/38, Hadith 6254, and "Sahih Muslim", Vol.3/1422, Hadith 1798.

al-Basri is reported to have said, "If you happen to pass by a group of people, some of whom are Muslims and some of whom are disbelievers, greet them."[47]

Ibn al-Qayyim said, "In this case (when you are allowed to greet them), then say 'Salamu Alayka' only. Do not invoke Allah's blessings on them, and address them in the singular. As for returning their greetings, opinions differ. The majority say that this is proper, while a minority maintain that it is not required that you respond to them, as it is neither required that you should respond to *Ahl al-Bidah*. The more correct position is the first. The difference being that we are ordered to keep away from *Ahl al-Bidah*, to strengthen ourselves against them and be cautious of them, but this is not the case with *'Ahl adh-Dhimmah'*."[48]

The view of the majority, that one is obliged to respond to the greetings of the People of the Book, is supported by the Hadith: "When the Jews greet you, they usually say, 'As-Saamu Alaykum' (Death be on you), so you should say (in reply to them), 'Wa Alaykum' (And on you)."[49] Also the Prophet ﷺ said, "If the people of the Scripture greet you, then you should say (in reply), 'Wa Alaykum'."[50]

---

[47] *"Tafsir al-Qurtubi"*, Vol.11/112.
[48] *"Zaad al-Maa'd"*, Vol.2/425.
[49] "Sahih al-Bukhari", Vol.11/42, Hadith 6257, and "Sahih Muslim", Vol.4/1705, Hadith 2164.
[50] "Sahih al-Bukhari", Vol.11/42, Hadith 6258, and "Sahih Muslim", Vol.4/1705, Hadith 2163.

Section Three: Benefit from the Disbelievers and from their Resources

Islam permits Muslims to approach non-Muslims in order to benefit from their knowledge of: chemistry, physics, medicine, manufacturing, agriculture, management and so forth, when these sorts of useful knowledge have not been acquired by pious Muslims.[51]

We are allowed to ask them for directions, to buy arms and clothing from them and to make use of the things which they have of which we have some need. Thus Muslims and non-Muslims may benefit equally from these things. A Muslim is not, however, at liberty to interpret aspects of his faith, elements of his religion, the meaning of the Qur'an or the Sunnah, the elements of our Islamic social or political system, or matters of Islamic etiquette and custom, under the influence of non-Muslims.[52]

We have already spoken about the error into which Muslims fell, when they adopted Greek philosophy and the asceticism of the Hindus and Zoroastrians, since these things, when they become mixed up with Islam, obscure its doctrine and distort its message. But it was right to have translated the books of medicine and chemistry and the new sciences; this is what led them to discover algebra. The Islamic intellect,

---

[51] *"Maa'lim Fi at-Tareeq"*, p.131-132, and *"Majmu' Fatawa"*, Vol.4/114.
[52] *"Maa'lim Fi at-Tareeq"*, p.131.

enlightened by the Revelation of Allah, is fully capable of discovery and innovation in all fields of science, the arts and literature. This is because faith is an asset, to every Muslim, in this quest. In it, the benefits of hard work and perseverance are demonstrated. The advances Muslims made, in the past, were not to benefit them alone. Indeed, all people benefited from them. Europe was, for centuries, dependent upon the science which the Muslims excelled. The situation has now been reversed, and the West has taken up the scientific leadership world, while the Muslims sleep. No longer are we at the forefront of inquiry and discovery. Indeed, the current generation now depend upon the students of their grandparents who have now become their teachers.

It is encouraging to see that today Islam is spreading everywhere; Muslims should be aware of what to adopt from other people, in order to enjoy some benefit from it, and what to leave aside, in order to avoid repeating the errors of the past. In order to do this we will have to put the greatest emphasis on our Islamic Creed, and allow ourselves to be guided by it, to re-build Islam from a basic foundation. Then, we will be in the position again to borrow what we need from the non-Muslims, but with caution and discrimination. Then, our science will be shaped in the light of sound belief, and not in the shadow of atheism and blind materialism.

One might ask what scientific methods of research have to do with religion. The answer is that there is no separation of religion from science. Indeed, Islam is the religion of science. The elaboration of a scientific method, based upon sound Islamic principles, instills in the heart a deeply rooted faith in the Omnipotence of the Creator: in the infinite Magnitude of His Creation, the evidence of His Perfect Creation is to be found at every level of existence.

However, the opposition betrays a striking inconsistency, for while the proponents of 'modern scientific method' claim neutrality, we see that it is quite impossible to maintain this position while advancing the theoretical claims of Marx, Freud or Durkenheim. Unlike Muslims who deal with these modern scientific methods, while at the same time saying that they believe in the Creed of One God, as conveyed by the luminary vision of Muhammad Ibn Abdullah ﷺ.

This fact is plain for all to see. No one could deny it other than the arrogant or the foolish, both of whom are incapable of recognizing that they are only wronging themselves.

This position, that one is allowed to profit from the knowledge of the disbelievers, is supported by the practice of the Prophet ﷺ. There is a Hadith which has been related by Al-Bukhari and others in, "The Book of Hiring", in the chapter: 'The employment of pagans (by Muslims) if necessary, or if no Muslims are available for that purpose', in which Aishah narrated: "The Prophet ﷺ and Abu Bakr ﷺ employed a (pagan) man from the tribe of Ad-Dail and the tribe of 'Abd bin 'Adi, as a guide. He was an expert guide and he broke the oath contract which he had to abide by with the tribe of Al-Asi Bin Wa'il and he was on the religion of Quraish pagans. The Prophet ﷺ and Abu Bakr ﷺ had confidence in him, gave him their riding camels and told him to bring them to the cave of Thaur after three days. So, he brought them their two riding camels after three days, and both of them (The Prophet ﷺ and Abu Bakr ﷺ) set out accompanied by Amir Ibn Fuhairah and the Dili guide who guided them, below Makkah, along the road leading to the sea-shore."[53]

Ibn al-Qayyim said: "The name of this guide was Abdullah Ibn Uraiqit ad-Duali. He was hired for this purpose, despite his disbelief. This proves that it is permitted to seek the advice and assistance of the disbelievers in medical and commercial matters and other such things which do not involve establishing a dependence upon them, mutual or otherwise. It proves that the mere fact that a person is a disbeliever is not sufficient grounds for you to totally avoid contact with him. Indeed, nothing could be more important than the choice of a guide through a dangerous country, and especially if one is fleeing from an enemy."[54]

Ibn Bataal said: Most of the jurists permit the hiring of pagans, whether or not it is a matter of necessity, so long as the hired person is subordinate to the Muslim there is no harm. The Muslim, however, is not permitted to work as employee for pagans, because he will place himself under the disbeliever's authority.[55]

---

[53] "Sahih al-Bukhari", Vol.4/442, Hadith 2263.
[54] "Bada'i' al-Fawaa'd", Vol.3/208.
[55] "Fath al-Bari", Vol.4/442.

But, what would be the response to the question, may a Muslim hire himself to a disbeliever?

In fact, we can find an answer to this too in Sahih Al-Bukhari: Al-Khabbab ۞ narrated [56]: "I was a blacksmith and did some work for Al-'Aas Ibn Wa'il. When he owed me some money for my work, I went to him to ask for that due amount. He said, 'I will not pay you unless you disbelieve in Muhammad,' I said, 'By Allah! I will never do that until you die and are resurrected.' He said, 'Will I be dead and be resurrected after my death?' I replied, 'Yes.' He said, 'There I will have property and offspring, so then I will pay you your due.' (At this) Allah ۞ revealed the verse,

Have you seen him who disbelieved in Our revelations saying: Surely I shall be given wealth and children (if I will be alive again)[57]

Al-Muhallab said: 'Scholars have discouraged Muslims from entering into the service of disbelievers in a land of war. But, if this is unavoidable then he may do so under two conditions; if whatever he is engaged in is permitted to Muslims; and that it does not hurt other Muslims.' [58]

---

[56] "Sahih al-Bukhari", Vol.4/452, Hadith 2275, "The Book of Hiring", Chapter: Is it permissible for a Muslim to work as employee for pagans in a land of war?
[57] *Maryam*: 77.
[58] *"Fath al-Bari"*, Vol.4/452.

As for hiring pagan mercenaries in battles, it is prohibited. Muslim reported a Hadith, on the authority of Aishah, who said, "The Messenger of Allah ﷺ set out for Badr. When he reached Harrat al-Wabarah (a place four miles from Madinah), a man met him who was known for his valour and courage. The Companions of the Messenger of Allah ﷺ were pleased to see him. He said, 'I have come so that I may follow you and receive a share of the booty.' The Messenger of Allah ﷺ said to him, 'Do you believe in Allah and His Apostle?' He said. 'No.' The Messenger of Allah ﷺ said: 'Go back, for I shall not seek help from a *Mushrik* (polytheist).' He went on until we reached Shajarah, where the man met him again. He asked him the same question again and the man gave him the same answer. He said: 'Go back, I shall not seek help from a *Mushrik*.' The man returned and overtook him in the desert. He asked him as he had done previously; 'Do you believe in Allah and His Apostle?' The man said: 'Yes.' The Messenger of Allah ﷺ told him: 'Then come with us.'"[59]

However, according to Al-Haazimi[60], scholars are not in agreement on this point. One group have said that it is forbidden to seek this sort of assistance from disbelievers, and base their assertion on the literal interpretation of this Hadith. They have said that the

---

[59] "Sahih Muslim", Vol.3/1499, Hadith 1817.

[60] His full name is: Imam Abu Bakr Muhammad Ibn Musa' Ibn Uthman Ibn Hazim, known as Al-Haazimi, originally from Hamadhan, and a scholar in Hadith. He was born in 548 A.H. but died, in Baghdad, in 584 A.H. See Az-Zarkali's *"Al-I'laam"*, Vol.7/117, Fourth Edition.

account is confirmed and that evidence to the contrary cannot compare to it in terms of its soundness or its authenticity. They dismiss the assertion that it was later abrogated. Another group have said that it is the right of the Imam to permit disbelievers to participate in a common military exercise with them, and indeed to seek their assistance in such an endeavour, provided that two conditions are met:

The first is that the Muslims should be so few in numbers as to be constrained by necessity to seek this assistance,

The second is that these people (disbelievers) should be trustworthy and reliable, posing no threat to dominate the Muslims.

If either of these two conditions is not met then the Imam may not permit such assistance from the disbelievers, if they are met then this is permitted. The evidence for this is contained in an account related by Ibn Abbas ﷻ who says that the Prophet ﷺ accepted assistance from the Jews of the tribe of Qaynuqaa', and that he accepted the help of Safwan Ibn Umayyah, to fight Hawaazaan, at the Battle of Hunayn. Because this was after the Battle of Badr they say that it demonstrates that the earlier account of Aishah was abrogated by it.[61] Al-Haazimi added that there is no harm in accepting the help of the pagans against the pagans, as long as they participate voluntarily and have no share in the booty.[62]

---

[61] Al-Haazimi: *"Al-I'tibaar Fi an-Na'sikh wal-Mansukh Mina al-Aathaar"*, p.219.
[62] Ibid., p.220.

Ibn al-Qayyim adopts this position, in his discussion of the benefits of Treaty of Hudaybiyyah, saying, "It is permitted to accept the assistance of reliable people from among the disbelievers in *Jihad*, if this is really necessary, since the Prophet ﷺ accepted the help of al-Khuza'ee, even though he was a pagan at the time. There is an element of good in this as it is better to allow him to continue to associate himself with the enemy and thereby gather information for the benefit of Muslims."[63]

Ibn al-Qayyim also said that among the lessons of the Battle of Hunayn was that the Imam may make use of the disbelievers' weapons and personnel in order to confront the enemy, as the Prophet ﷺ also borrowed the armour of Safwan Ibn Umayyah even though he was at the time a disbeliever.[64]

Muhammad Ibn Abdul Wahhab concurs with this saying, "There are no grounds for the censure of one who makes use of the disbelievers in some matters relating to (the advancement) of the faith. This is proven by the story of al-Khuza'ee."[65]

To conclude this discussion, we can say that it is allowed for one to seek benefit from the disbelievers and from the knowledge which they possess; this is but the fruit of human endeavour. This position is well supported

---

[63] *"Zaad al-Maa'd"*, Vol.3/301, and the story of al-Khuza'ee is in *"Taareekh at-Tabari"*, Vol.2/625.
[64] *"Zaad al-Maa'd"*, Vol.3/479, and the story is in *"Seerat Ibn Hisham"*, Vol.4/83, and in *"Taareekh at-Tabari"*, Vol.3/73.
[65] Muhammad Ibn Abdul Wahhab, *"Mulhaq Musannafaat"*, p.7.

as we have seen above, for there is further evidence of this in the account of the contract the that Prophet ﷺ had with some Jews to farm and cultivate the land of Khaybar, and be given half of its yield.[66]

Muslims are also permitted to enter into the service of disbelievers, so long as there is no suggestion of deference to their religion or prejudices, and no danger of submission to them nor subjugation by them. Seeking their help in war is also permitted provided the Imam of the Muslims sees in this some benefit for the Muslim community, otherwise it is not permitted.

However, one should exercise caution in employing disbelievers in the service of Muslims. One is not allowed to employ them in any position of public responsibility, such as in the civil service, since this is an affront to Islam and to the Muslims. What is more, it is in blatant contravention of the Shar'iah; a challenge to its authority, and a humiliation to Muslims, despite those who imagine that it is permissible to employ them in such places. There are a number of relevant reports about this:

One of these is related by Imam Ahmad with a Sound *Isnad*. He quotes Abu Musa al-Ash'aree ﷺ, who says, "I told Omar ﷺ that I had a Christian secretary. He said, 'What is the matter with you? May Allah strike you down! Did you not hear that Allah has said, **⟨O you who believe! Take not the Jews and the Christians for**

---

[66] This Hadith is in "Sahih al-Bukhari", Vol.5/15, Hadith 2331, The Book of Agriculture, Chapter: Share-cropping with the Jews.

friends, they are but friends to one another〉 (5:51)
Why don't you take a Muslim secretary?' I said,
'Commander of the Faithful, he is only my secretary, his
religion is his affair.' He said 'Do not show them respect
after Allah has disgraced them. Do not honour them after
Allah has humiliated them. Do not draw them to us after
Allah has repelled them from us.'"[67]

Omar ﷺ also wrote to Abu Hurayrah saying,
"...and do not employ disbelievers in any position of
responsibility for Muslims' affairs. Occupy yourself with
the welfare of the Muslims, as you are one of them,
however Allah has chosen to place their burdens upon
your shoulders."[68]

Omar Ibn Abdul Aziz, may Allah have Mercy
upon him, wrote to one of his governors saying, "It has
come to my attention that you have employed a Christian
secretary who has been given responsibility for the
affairs of Muslims. Yet Allah ﷻ has said, 〈O you who
believe! Take not for helpers those who take your
religion for mockery and fun from among those who
received the Scripture before you, nor from among
the disbelievers; and fear Allah if you indeed are true
believers〉 (5: 57). If you receive my letter, invite (your
secretary) Hassaan Ibn Zayd to Islam. If he accepts then
he is one of us and we are with him, but if he refuses then

---

[67] Ibn Taymiyyah had mentioned this Hadith in "*Iqtidaa' as-Siraat al-Mustaqeem*", p. 50 and said that is is related by Imam Ahmad, but I could not find it in "*Musnad Abee Musa*". Al-Bayhaqi mentioned it in "*As-Sunan al-Kubra*'", 10/127.
[68] "*Ahkaam Ahl adh-Dhimma*", Vol.1/212.

dismiss him and do not give responsibility for the affairs of Muslims to anyone other than a Muslim again. Hassaan Ibn Zayd embraced Islam and was exemplary in his religion.[69]

In the days of the Abbasids, when it became common to employ the people of the Scripture in the affairs of Muslims, one of the scholars, Shabib Ibn Shaybah, rose to the challenge to confront this practice. He went to see Abu Ja'far al-Mansur, who received him, and said, "Commander of the Faithful! Be mindful of your duty to Allah, for this is advice given to you for His Sake. I find myself before you, with but one desire: to offer my sincere and humble advice to you, and to express my concern for your welfare and that Allah's Blessings may be upon you. May Allah strengthen your hand, fill your breast with mercy and make your name known. O Commander of the Faithful! There is within this house a dark spectre which casts its long shadow of oppression; an unjust spirit whose business is other than the Book of Allah and the Sunnah of His Prophet, ﷺ.

O Commander of the Faithful! *Ahl adh-Dhimmah* are beginning to rule over the Muslims, oppressing them and riding roughshod over them. They try to seize their lands, confiscate their wealth, oppressing yet asserting that it is upon your authority that they act, to justify their unbridled greed. These people will never benefit you before Allah, on the Day of Resurrection." Then al-Mansour replied, "...Contact my officers and dismiss those of them who are *Dhimmi*, however, you may

---

[69] *"Ahkaam Ahl adh-Dhimma"*, Vol.1/214.

employ whomsoever Shabib approves." But then Shabib said, "Commander of the Faithful, no Muslim will enter your service so long as these disbelievers remain; for were they to obey these disbelievers they would anger Allah. Yet, if they were to disobey these disbelievers, they would incite you against Muslims. Therefore, by accepting one of them, you accept all of them as a whole. Everyday you should employ a Muslim, but get rid of a disbeliever."[70]

In Short, we should make a distinction between employment of disbelievers in a particular job, and putting them in positions of power over Muslims, or influence, in an Islamic state. Ordinarily, it is permitted to employ them as we have discussed above. But it is not allowed to put them into positions which would contradict the spirit of the law, the fundamental principle being that the Word of Allah should be supreme, the word of the disbelievers should be the lowermost.

It is preferable that Muslims should depend upon their own resources, so that the nation would remain uniquely Islamic, as Allah has ordained. We ask Almighty Allah to hasten the day when Muslims would return to their true faith; then they will be rid of the disbelievers' influence which entered into all of their affairs. Allah's power encompasses all things.

---

[70] *"Shadharaat adh-Dhahab"*, Vol.1/215.

TAQIYAH and IKRAAH (Dissimulation and Coercion)

The ruling regarding these two points are mentioned in the Shari'ah. They both illustrate the limits of force which Muslims are expected to tolerate.

TAQIYAH: (Dissimulation):

Ibn Mas'ud ﷺ has said that: *Taqiyah* is saying a thing with the tongue while your heart remains reassured in faith.[71] Abu al-'Aaliyyah said: '*Taqiyah* is in word but not in deed.'[72] Ibn Hajar al-'Asqalaani said, '*Taqiyah* is to keep what is in the heart (belief) from public view.'[73] Sayyid Qutb said, '*Taqiyah* is with the tongue but is not bonded to the heart, nor by deed. In it there is no license for affection of the believer for the disbeliever; so no believer may come to the assistance of a disbeliever, as this is not permitted; for there is no deception before Allah.'[74]

When is *Taqiyah* permitted?

Allah ﷻ has said,
Let not the believers take the disbelievers as friends instead of the believers, and whoever does that will never be helped by Allah in any way, except if you fear a danger from them.

[71] "*Tafseer at-Tabari*", Vol.3/228-229.
[72] Ibid., Vol.3/228-229.
[73] "*Fath al-Bari*", Vol.12/314.
[74] "*Ad-Dilaal*", Vol.1/386.

And Allah warns you against Himself (His Punishment), and to Allah is the final return [75]

Al-Baghawi said: "Allah ﷻ has prohibited the believers from taking the disbelievers as friends and protectors, and from disregarding the disbelievers' true nature; except when the disbelievers should dominate over them and force them to accept them, or if the Muslim, finding himself among them, is in fear of them and so influences them with his tongue, while his heart maintains the faith. Thus, he defends himself but stops short of endangering the life or property of Muslims or of exposing them to danger. *Taqiyah* is only permitted on fear of death, and with a purity of intention. Allah has said, **❴Except him who is forced thereto and whose heart is at rest with Faith❵** (**16:106**). Even though this is a license, for one who is patient, even unto death, his reward would be great indeed." [76]

Ibn al-Qayyim said, "It is well known that *Taqiyah* is not a license to take the disbelievers as intimates. Indeed, when association with the disbelievers was forbidden, it became necessary to take them as enemies and to distance oneself from them. One should declare his enmity for them, at every opportunity, but if he should fear reprisals from them, then he may hide his enmity for them, although *Taqiyah* does not mean to be in association with them." [77]

---

[75] *Aal-Imran*: 28.
[76] *"Tafseer al-Baghawi"*, Vol.1/336, and al-Jassaas's *"Ahkaam al-Qur'an"*, Vol.2/289.
[77] *"Bada'i' al-Fawa'id"*, Vol.3/69.

However, while *Taqiyah* provides an easy opportunity for Satan to deceive one who is weak or has some darkness in the heart, into some forbidden commerce with the enemies of Allah - Allah said after that: ❨**And Allah warns you against Himself (His Punishment), and to Allah is the final return**❩. Allah warns about taking this as an easy solution and falling into the trap of allying oneself to the enemies of Allah. He warns one that it is unto Him that one is bound, so one would find one's reward for what one used to do in this world. One should not imagine that one could commit any grave error in this world, fooling oneself or others that one could be spared Allah's Punishment in the Hereafter.[78]

Ibn Jarir At-Tabari remarks in his discussion of the verse, ❨**except if you fear a danger from them**❩, saying that it means, 'except if you find yourself under their authority and fear for your lives.' So you may show them friendship with your tongues, but guard your enmity for them secretly and do not encourage them in their disbelief nor assist them against any Muslim.[79]

---

[78] *"Diraasaat Qur'aaniyya"*, p.326-327.
[79] *"Tafseer at-Tabari"*, Vol.3/228.

Allah ﷻ has said:

Whoever disbelieved in Allah after his belief, except him who is forced thereto and whose heart is at rest with Faith - but such as open their breasts to disbelief, - on them is wrath from Allah, and theirs will be a great torment. That is because they loved and preferred the life of this world over that of the Hereafter. And Allah guides not the people who disbelieve[80]

Ibn Abbas ؓ said: The first verse was revealed about Ammaar Ibn Yaasir, after the pagans had arrested him, his father, his mother, Sumayyah, together with Suhaib, Bilal, Khabab and Saalim. They tied Sumayyah between two camels and struck her with a lance, killing her. Her husband Yaasir was also killed. They were the first two Muslims, ever, to have been killed for their faith. As for Ammaar, he complied with them by saying what they compelled him to say. Then the Prophet ﷺ was informed that Ammaar had renounced his Islam. The Prophet ﷺ said, 'Certainly not. Ammaar is a pillar of faith, from head to toe. Faith is in his blood and in his bones.'[81] Then Ammaar came to the Prophet ﷺ and wept. The Prophet ﷺ dried his tears and said, 'If they ever do

---

[80] *An-Nahl*: 106-107.
[81] The wording of this Hadith in this manner is incorrect, the sound wording is narrated by Al-Hakim in his *"Mustadrak"*, Vol.3/392-393, and by An-Nasa'i', Vol.8/111.

that again, do just what you have done.'[82] Then Allah revealed this verse.[83]

At-Tabari explains that the meaning of the verse is, that those who are forced to say a word of disbelief, with their tongues, while their hearts are reassured with faith, are free of disbelief. They are certain of truth, and faithful to their resolve. But whoever disbelieves in Allah, after faith, brings the Wrath of Allah upon himself, and will pay a terrible price for his choice of disbelief, rejection of faith, and willing submission to the unbelievers.[84] Ibn Kathir explains that this was because they preferred the life of this world to the Hereafter; and so it was only for the state of this world that they renounced their faith.[85]

Conditions of Coercion

Ibn Hajr mentions four conditions which must be met before one could claim to have been coerced:

(1) That the person who threatens you is capable of carrying out his threat, and the person who is threatened is incapable of defending himself, even by flight.

---

[82] Hadith *Mursal*, see: *"Fath al-Ba'ri"*, Vol.12/312.
[83] Al-Waahidi, *"Asbaab an-Nuzul"*, p.162, *"Tafseer at-Tabari"*, Vol.14/182, and *"Tafseer Ibn Kathir"*, Vol.4/525.
[84] *"Tafseer at-Tabari"*, Vol.14/182.
[85] *"Tafseer Ibn Kathir"*, Vol.4/525.

(2) He must be certain that if he fails to comply the threat will be carried out.

(3) The threat must be immediate. If someone says to you, 'If you don't do such and such, we shall strike you tomorrow', it would not be considered coercion. You may however comply with a threat to act against you in the 'very near future', or at the approach of a deadline which will not be ignored.

(4) If no alternative to compliance is apparent.

The majority of scholars do not make any distinction between verbal and physical coercion, but they exclude from one's accepted deeds anything that is prohibited, such as killing a soul without a just cause.[86]

Al-Khaazin said: "The coercion which the scholars have mentioned, excusing one from pronouncing a word of disbelief, is the threat of death, severe beating or torture. They are also agreed that someone who has been forced to declare disbelief may not make an open declaration, but he should resist this, giving his opponents the impression that he has already disbelieved. If they force him to announce this clearly and openly, then he may do so once his heart is fortified by faith, continuing to deny inwardly his declaration of disbelief. However, it is better for him to remain steadfast unto death. This is the lesson we have learned from Sumayyah

---

[86] *"Fath al-Ba'ri"*, Vol.12/311-312.

and Yaasir, and from the persistence of Bilal before the torture of his inquisitors."[87]

Bilal ﷺ continued to refuse to renounce his state of Islam, even after a huge stone was placed on his chest, as he was pinned down in the blazing sun. His torturers demanded that he deny the unity of Allah, but he only replied, 'Ahad, Ahad, i.e., 'One, One', and then said, 'By Allah, if I knew a word more odious to you than this I would say it!'[88]

Similarly, Habib Ibn Zayd al-Ansari[89], when Musaylimah al-Kadaab asked him, 'Do you say Muhammad is the Messenger of Allah?' replied, 'Yes'. Musaylimah said, 'Do you testify that I am the messenger of Allah!' But Habib continued to say, 'I do not hear this' as Musaylamah cut him up.'[90]

Also there is the example of the Companion, Abdullah Ibn Hudhaafa as-Sahami, who was taken hostage by the Romans. They brought him before their king who said, 'Convert to Christianity, and I shall give you a share in my kingdom, and my daughter in marriage.' Abdullah replied, 'If you were to give me all that you possess and all that the Arabs possess, I would

---

[87] "Tafseer al-Khaazin", Vol.4/117.

[88] "Tafseer Ibn Kathir", Vol.4/525.

[89] Habib Ibn Zayd Ibn A'sim Ibn Amru Al-Ansari, the brother of Abdullah Ibn Zayd, was mentioned by Ibnu Ishaaq among those who were at al-Aqabah. He was killed by Musaylimah. Ibnu Sa'd said: Habib participated in the Battles of Uhud, al-Khandaq, and others, see: "Al-Isa'bah", Vol.1/307.

[90] "Tafseer Ibn Kathir", Vol.4/525.

not renounce the religion of Muhammad, for an instant.' The King said, 'Then you are a dead man.' 'So be it,' said Abdullah. So they took him and hung him up on a cross. Then marksmen were called to shoot their arrows, grazing his hands and his legs, and all the while they called him to adopt their religion which he still refused to accept. Then they cut him down and brought a huge copper pot, which they heated up. They brought one of their Muslim prisoners whom they threw into the pot, before Abdullah, soon he was roasted to bones. They threatened him with the same, but still he refused. Then they brought a block and tackle, to winch him up and throw him in the pot, but when they were about to throw him in he began to weep. This sparked some hope in the heart of the king, so he asked him again, to which he replied, 'I was crying because I have but one life to sacrifice for the Sake of Allah. O, that I should have as many as the numbers of hairs on my head, to be tormented in this way, for the Sake of Allah!

In another account he is said to have been imprisoned and deprived of food and drink for a number of days. But when they sent him wine and pork, he did not go near it. Then they summoned him and asked, 'Why don't you eat?' 'While it is allowed for me to eat this, I fear that I would then feel badly toward you for it,' he said. The king said: 'kiss my head and I will set you free.' Abdullah said, 'And you will also set free all the Muslim hostages.' The king agreed. Abdullah kissed his head and the king set him free with all the Muslim hostages he had taken. When he returned Omar ibn al-Khattab said, 'Every Muslim should kiss the head of

Adbullah Ibn Hudhaafah, and I will be the first to do so. Then he rose and kissed his head.[91]

Aspects of Coercion

(1) Force may drive one to seek refuge. In the face of persecution you may take refuge in your heart but take no pleasure in this, in the absence of any alternative. This is the context in which the verse was revealed: **《Whoever disbelieved in Allah after his belief, except him who is forced thereto and whose heart is at rest with Faith》**.

(2) Force may take the form of threats. When someone capitulates under threats, although acting against his will, an element of choice remains. Choosing the lesser of two evils is an illustration of this. Thus Shu'aib ﷺ chose between returning to disbelief or exile from his homeland:

> **The chiefs of those who were arrogant among his people said: "We shall certainly drive you out, O Shu'aib, and those who have believed with you from our town, unless you return to our religion." He said: "Even though we hate it! "We should have invented a lie against Allah if we returned to your religion, after Allah has rescued us from it. It is not for us to return to it unless Allah, our Lord, should (so) will. Our Lord comprehends all things in His**

---

[91] *"Tafseer Ibn Kathir"*, Vol.4/526.

Knowledge. In Allah do we put our trust. Our Lord! Judge between us and our people in truth, for You are the Best of those who give judgment [92]

Therefore, it is not permitted to accept such coercion (to return to disbelief). This is also supported by another verse:

Of mankind are some who say: "We believe in Allah," but, if they are made to suffer for the sake of Allah, they consider the trial of mankind as Allah's Punishment; and then, if victory comes from your Lord, (the hypocrites) will say: "Verily! We were with you (helping you)". Is not Allah Best Aware of what is in the breast of the *Aalameen* (mankind and Jinns) [93]

(3) Force can break the morally weak. In this case there may be no threat nor persecution, but the feeble will fall under the weight of obligation placed upon him by his peers. This is what happened to those Muslims who remained in Makkah after the *Hijrah*. Because of their inability to either defend their position or leave, they found themselves with no alternatives, though had they been able to overcome this dilemma they would have

---

[92] *Al-A'raf*: 88-89.
[93] *Al-Ankabut*: 10

done so, regardless of the cost. Allah has forgiven such people.[94]

Ibn Atiq has spoken earlier about the position with regard to those who had been able either to resist or to leave, but did not do so, preferring to suffer the consequences. Here, he cited Ibn Taymiyyah as his authority, 'I have studied various opinions and found that coercion varies according to the coerced person. Accordingly, the coercion which brings with it a declaration of disbelief is not the same as that allowed in *Hiba* (gifts donated freely), because as Imam Ahmad had mentioned, on many occasions, coercion can only be an excuse for someone who has been subjected to persecution or torture. Simple words have no power to force disbelief.[95]

Final word about Coercion

It is important to point out the difference between coercion and the feeling of fear, which is associated with the hope and awe, both of which are aspects of worship. So too, we should distinguish between weakness and lack of moral fibre; between submission to the enemy and inclining towards him, the loss of heart and the abandonment of reliance and trust in Allah. Everyone has within himself an inner source of strength ,on which to draw, according to the circumstances. This enables him

---

[94] Abdul Majid Ash-Shaadhili, *"Haddu al-Islam Wa Haqiqatu al-Eemaan"*, p.523-526.
[95] Ibnu Ateeq, *"Ad-Difa'"*, p.30.

to reject anything in the privacy of his heart. The Prophet ﷺ called this '*Jihad*' when he said, "..whoever fights them with his heart, is a believer. But beyond this, there remains not a mustard seed's weight of faith."[96]

It is therefore imperative to resist the oppressive ruler and the alliance which he demands; even if he has the power to persuade you, otherwise, he can not be allowed to influence your heart. Allah addressed the believers, after the events at Uhud, thus,

> **And with how many a prophet have there been a number of devoted men who fought (beside him). They quailed not for aught that befell them in the Way of Allah, nor did they weaken, nor were they brought low. Allah loves the steadfast. Their cry was only that they said: Our Lord! Forgive us for our sins and wasted efforts, make our foothold sure, and give us victory over the disbelieving folk. So Allah gave them the reward of the world and good reward of the Hereafter. Allah loves those whose deeds are good. O you who believe! If you obey those who disbelieve, they will make you turn back on your heels, and you turn back as losers. But Allah is your Protector, and He is the best of helpers.** [97]

Abdullah Ibn Mas'oud ﷺ said, "It is enough for Allah to see the heart of one who has seen a

---

[96] "Sahih Muslim", Vol.1/70, Hadith 50, The *Book of Eemaan*.
[97] *Aal-Imraan*: 146-150.

reprehensible action, and could not do anything other than to be resentful at it." That you distance yourself from it, and not to lend yourself to it, is proof of your having been resentful. The heart should show superiority towards internal defeat. By the strength of the heart you may refuse falsehood, regardless of the arrogance and pride of those who would force you to submit to them. By this strength, you may withdraw from them within and deny their right on you. This is *Jihad* of the heart; it is a *Jihad* which has its deepest effect on the life of man.[98]

---

[98] Abdul Majid Ash-Shaadhili, "*Haddu al-Islam Wa Haqiqatu al-Eemaan*", p.527-528.

Winning *the* Heart *of your* Wife

Ibraahim Ibn Saaleh al-Mahmud

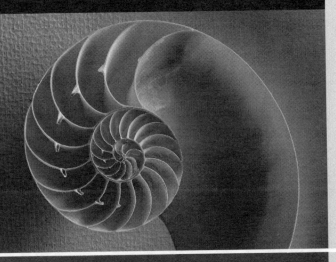

AL-FIRDOUS

ENJOINING GOOD FORBIDDING EVIL

SHEIKH AL-ISLAM IBN TAIMIYYAH

Al-Wala'
Wa'l-Bara'

According to the
'Aqeedah of the Salaf

PART 4

Muhammad Saeed
al-Qahtani

Al-Firdous Ltd., London